ANTHOLOGY OF GOETHE SONGS

RECENT RESEARCHES IN THE MUSIC OF THE NINETEENTH AND EARLY TWENTIETH CENTURIES

Rufus Hallmark, general editor

A-R Editions, Inc., publishes seven series of musicological editions that present music brought to light in the course of current research:

Recent Researches in the Music of the Middle Ages and Early Renaissance
Charles M. Atkinson, general editor

Recent Researches in the Music of the Renaissance
James Haar, general editor

Recent Researches in the Music of the Baroque Era
Christoph Wolff, general editor

Recent Researches in the Music of the Classical Era
Eugene K. Wolf, general editor

Recent Researches in the Music of the Nineteenth and Early Twentieth Centuries
Rufus Hallmark, general editor

Recent Researches in American Music
H. Wiley Hitchcock, general editor

Recent Researches in the Oral Traditions of Music
Philip V. Bohlman, general editor

Each *Recent Researches* edition is devoted to works
by a single composer or to a single genre of composition.
The contents are chosen for their potential interest to scholars
and performers, then prepared for publication according to the
standards that govern the making of all reliable historical editions.

Subscribers to any of these series, as well as patrons of subscribing institutions,
are invited to apply for information about the "Copyright-Sharing Policy"
of A-R Editions, Inc., under which policy any part of an edition
may be reproduced free of charge for study or performance.

For information contact

A-R EDITIONS, INC.
801 Deming Way
Madison, Wisconsin 53717

(608) 836-9000

RECENT RESEARCHES IN THE MUSIC OF THE NINETEENTH
AND EARLY TWENTIETH CENTURIES • VOLUME 23

ANTHOLOGY OF GOETHE SONGS

Edited by Richard D. Green

A-R Editions, Inc.
Madison

To
John Buccheri

© 1994 by A-R Editions, Inc.
All Rights Reserved
Printed in the United States of America

Library of Congress Cataloging-in-Publication Data

Anthology of Goethe songs / edited by Richard D. Green.
   1. score. — (Recent researches in the music of the nineteenth and
early twentieth centuries ; v. 23)
    "Texts and translations": p.
    Includes bibliographical references.
    Contents: Sehnsucht / Carl Zelter — Das Blümlein Wunderschön /
Johann Rudolf Zumsteeg — Nähe des Geliebten ; Das Veilchen / Wenzel
Johann Tomaschek —Die Spinnerinn / Ferdinand Ries — Mignons Lied /
Ludwig Spohr — Der Fischer / Moritz Hauptmann — Der Erlkönig /
Bernhard Klein — Der König von Thule / Heinrich Marschner — Der
Zauberlehrling / Carl Loewe — Nähe des Geliebten / Ferdinand Hiller
— Wonne der Wehmut / Robert Franz — Clärchens Lied / Anton
Rubinstein — Freisinn / Hans von Bülow — Nachtgesang / Joseph
Rheinberger — Wer sich der Einsamkeit ergibt ; Am Flusse / Arnold
Mendelssohn — Lied des Mephistopheles / Ferruccio Busoni — Mailied
/ Hans Pfitzner — An den Mond / Justus Hermann Wetzel — Geweihter
Platz / Nikolay Karlovich Medtner — Rastlose Liebe / Othmar
Schoeck.
    ISBN 0-89579-307-5
    1. Songs with piano. 2. Goethe, Johann Wolfgang von, 1749–1832-
-Musical settings. I. Green, Richard D., 1944– . II. Series.
M2.R23834   vol. 23
[M1619.5.G56]   94-39434
                                              CIP
                                               M

Contents

PREFACE		vii
Introduction		vii
The Lied in the Age of Goethe		vii
Goethe and the Lied		x
The Songs		xii
Composers and Musical Sources		xiii
Editorial Method		xxi
Critical Notes		xxii
Acknowledgments		xxiii
Notes		xxiv
TEXTS AND TRANSLATIONS		xxvi
PLATES		xxxix

The Songs

[1]	Sehnsucht "Nur wer die Sehnsucht kennt"	Carl Zelter	2
[2]	Das Blümlein Wunderschön "Ich kenn' ein Blümlein Wunderschön"	Johann Rudolf Zumsteeg	4
[3]	Nähe des Geliebten "Ich denke dein"	Wenzel Johann Tomaschek	8
[4]	Das Veilchen "Ein Veilchen auf der Wiese stand"	Wenzel Johann Tomaschek	12
[5]	Die Spinnerin "Als ich still und ruhig spann"	Ferdinand Ries	16
[6]	Mignons Lied "Kennst du das Land?"	Louis Spohr	19
[7]	Der Fischer "Das Wasser rauscht'"	Moritz Hauptmann	22
[8]	Der Erlkönig "Wer reitet so spät"	Bernhard Klein	31
[9]	Der König von Thule "Es war ein König in Thule"	Heinrich Marschner	39
[10]	Der Zauberlehrling "Hat der alte Hexenmeister"	Carl Loewe	43
[11]	Nähe des Geliebten "Ich denke dein"	Ferdinand Hiller	55
[12]	Wonne der Wehmut "Trocknet nicht"	Robert Franz	58
[13]	Clärchens Lied "Freudvoll"	Anton Rubinstein	60
[14]	Freisinn "Laßt mich nur auf meinem Sattel gelten!"	Hans von Bülow	63
[15]	Nachtgesang "O! gib vom weichen Pfühle"	Joseph Rheinberger	68
[16]	Wer sich der Einsamkeit ergibt	Arnold Mendelssohn	71
[17]	Am Flusse "Verfließet, vielgeliebte Lieder"	Arnold Mendelssohn	75
[18]	Lied des Mephistopheles "Es war einmal ein König"	Ferruccio Busoni	80
[19]	Mailied "Wie herrlich leuchtet"	Hans Pfitzner	86

[20] An den Mond "Füllest wieder Busch und Tal"	Justus Hermann Wetzel	92
[21] Geweihter Platz "Wenn zu den Reihen der Nymphen"	Nikolay Karlovich Medtner	97
[22] Rastlose Liebe "Dem Schnee, dem Regen"	Othmar Schoeck	102

Preface

Introduction

Few poets have had as profound and enduring an impact on the history of art music in Germany as has Johann Wolfgang von Goethe. As a poet, novelist, and playwright, Goethe was one of the most influential, insightful, and prodigious writers of his time. Since the late eighteenth century his dramatic works have provided a rich resource for the libretti of operas and singspiels, and over 700 of his verses have been set as solo lieder for voice and piano by nearly 600 composers. Unusually evocative in image and sensitive in sentiment, Goethe's poetry has inspired some of the most beautifully moving songs ever composed, and many are among the most familiar songs in all the modern repertoire.

While many are aware of the songs based on Goethe's poetry by well-known composers of the nineteenth century such as Schubert, Schumann, or Wolf, few have had the means to study the songs of these composers' contemporaries. A large amount of song literature of the nineteenth century by figures such as Tomaschek, Spohr, and Arnold Mendelssohn, much of it of musical as well as historical value, remains unknown.

Despite Goethe's significance to the history of German music and the wealth of scholarship on various aspects of his influence on music,[1] there have been few editions of lieder devoted exclusively to his poetry. Two useful anthologies compiled by Max Friedlaender are unfortunately no longer available. The volume *Gedichte von Goethe in Kompositionen seiner Zeitgenossen* (Weimar, 1896) contains works by composers of the late eighteenth and early nineteenth centuries, including Zelter, Reichardt, Zumsteeg, Eberwein, and Kayser; *Gedichte von Goethe in Kompositionen* (Weimar, 1916) is an anthology of settings by some of the major composers throughout the nineteenth century, such as Schubert, Schumann, Liszt, Brahms, and Strauss.

The present anthology contains twenty-two songs on Goethe's verses by significant yet lesser-known composers from the nineteenth and early twentieth centuries. This edition offers to performers and scholars a selection of Goethe's texts in settings by composers whose contribution to the history of lieder, however significant in their day, has since been largely ignored. This edition may also serve as a companion to two other anthologies in the series Recent Researches in the Music of the Nineteenth and Early Twentieth Centuries: *100 Years of Eichendorff Songs*, edited by Jurgen Thym, and *Famous Poets, Neglected Composers*, edited by J. W. Smeed. The prefaces to those volumes provide additional information on the history of the lied and on poetry in the nineteenth century.

Several composers represented in this volume, such as Zelter, Loewe, and Schoeck, enjoyed distinguished reputations during their lifetimes among musicians, critics, and the general public as sensitive composers of numerous, well-crafted lieder. Many other composers represented in this volume are known to modern audiences because of their contributions to genres other than song. Spohr and Pfitzner are distinguished for their instrumental and operatic works respectively, but are not generally recognized for their solo lieder. Students of nineteenth century music are acquainted with von Bülow through his association with Liszt and Wagner and his unalterable and influential advocacy of their music. Little, unfortunately, is known of his lieder, although many are entirely worthy examples of this genre from the New German School of the mid nineteenth century. Likewise, students of keyboard music are familiar with the names of Tomaschek and Busoni, yet while their position in the history of songs is important, few of their works in the genre are widely known.

The selection of lieder for this anthology was guided by a desire to include poems that are popular on their own and that are also known widely through the lieder of major figures. By comparative analyses we can often witness composers' divergent solutions to problems of text setting, gain insight into their poetic interpretation, and gather fresh meaning from the poem itself.[2] Zelter's setting of "Nur wer die Sehnsucht kennt" was probably known and approved by Goethe himself and is by itself an admirable song, but when compared to Schubert's setting of the same text, we readily see the liberties that the latter took with both the meaning and structure of the poem. Schubert's contribution to the history of the genre was not only to create lieder of inestimable value and sensitivity, greater than those of the previous generation, but in doing so he asserted his own reading of the poetry over that of the poet's. Not all composers of the nineteenth century followed this practice, for some, especially those later in the century (such as Wolf), were appreciably less proprietarian in their attitudes toward the literature they set.

The Lied in the Age of Goethe

In German-speaking provinces during the last two decades of the eighteenth century, lieder were only occasionally performed in public. The style of the genre was inappropriate to public performances at that time, and the tradition of commercial, public concerts was then still in its infancy. Songs from the later years of the eighteenth century were generally written in an intimate, folk-like style suited to small salon settings as

Hausmusik or directed toward specific occupations or social classes (such as the *Liedersammlung für Kinder und Kinderfreunde, Lieder für fröhliche Gesellschaften,* or *Sammlung von Freymäurerliedern,* all 1791). Within the early years of the nineteenth century, however, the *Lied* began to emerge among German-speaking lands as a genre capable of lofty artistic expression, written in a variety of forms and styles, and acceptable for public performance. But while the term *Lied* was loosely used by the middle of the nineteenth century as it is today, to mean simply a German song, many lexical definitions of the term during the same period acknowledged the older meaning of the word that had emerged during Goethe's life.

One reason for this dichotomy may stem from the fact that Goethe's poetry continued to be taken as the model for many definitions of the lied. For example, in the Brockhaus *Conversations-Lexikon* of 1835, *Lied* is defined as "a lyrical form of poetry, the simple poetic expression of a tender, self-contained feeling." The author claims that lieder are often set to music, and observes that:

> Among those [poems] that are later sung, only those of free and natural expression that produce a good sensation in a musical style and singable form can truly be considered a lied. The charming, agreeable and trivially superficial style, written in the French manner after Hagedorn, that was accepted for a while among the Germans as a feature of the lied, could not long be tolerated by German senses. The true lied need not avoid being profound. Such lieder were first restored to the Germans by Goethe, and it is no exaggeration to claim that since that time, recognition of the nature of lieder poetry has spread from Germany to the other literary cultures of Europe.[3]

During Goethe's life, the lied was recognized as a genre of both poetry and music and was defined either as a form of poetry appropriate for simple musical setting or as a genre of solo vocal music based on lyrical verses. The importance of this genre, which was among the most popular of all musical genres at the time, may be grasped when one realizes that during the latter years of the eighteenth century, vocal music was held as a model for all forms of composition. It is maintained, for example, in Johann Sulzer's influential *Allgemeine Theorie der schönen Künste* that "it is a fundamental rule that the composer's style be cantabile, that is singable, in vocal as well as in instrumental music. . . . If the composer wishes to be successful he himself must above all be able to sing."[4]

The two volumes of Sulzer's lexicon, containing essays on aspects of all the arts, were published in 1771 and 1774 and were soon widely known. Goethe was acquainted with the publication and, although he did not agree in all matters with Sulzer's conservative opinions, he nonetheless respected Sulzer's wisdom.[5] At the root of Sulzer's aesthetical principles is the ethical belief that all arts must emulate nature, and that by appealing to wholesome sentiments, the arts can edify man's behavior. In the discussion of the word *Lied*, Sulzer's lexicon stresses the importance of the simple and unaffected style of this genre, in which neither the artfulness of the singer nor the proficiency of the composer is emphasized. The simplicity of the lied did not prevent its touching the heart of the listener, "for it does not rely on amusing the ear, nor on artistic splendor, nor on surprises of artful harmonies and difficult modulations; rather merely on feeling."[6] Less a definition than a prescriptive description, the article on lied exhorts the composer to strive for complete unity between music (i.e., melody) and poetry.

The most important definition of the lied from the early years of the nineteenth century appears in the *Musikalisches Lexikon* of 1802 by the German theorist Heinrich Koch. Although the lexicon borrows information from Sulzer's *Allgemeine Theorie,* from which it quotes liberally, many of its entries are new. The dictionary was one of the most popular books of its kind (it was issued in many revisions during the nineteenth century) and was taken as a model for later terminological references on music. Koch's definition of *Lied,* which considers the term as a musical form of poetry, became typical in the first half of the century.

> With this term [*Lied*] one generally designates a lyrical poem of several strophes which is intended for song, and which is bound with a melody in such a way that it is repeated in each strophe. At the same time, it has the characteristic that it can be performed by everyone who has a healthy and flexible voice, without concern for artistic training. It follows from this that the melody of a lied may have neither so wide a range in notes, nor require such a manner of singing and prosody that distinguish the trained and experienced voices of arias. The expression of the emotions contained in the text is to be achieved, rather, through more appropriately simple means.[7]

This definition clearly suggests several salient features of lieder from this period. According to Koch, the lied was a genre of poetry specifically intended for strophic song, composed in a simple, personal style that could be sung comfortably by an amateur voice; its goal was the expression of the feelings suggested by the text. Although Koch does not discuss the nature of the accompaniment, we might conjecture, based on the citation above and on existing musical sources, that it was also to be simple, unobtrusive, and largely in the service of the poem. This attitude toward the relationship of music to text was typical for many musicians and poets, including Goethe himself, during the early nineteenth century.

At the end of the eighteenth century the lied was commonly distinguished from other styles of song and other forms of poetry. Although also a strophic poem, the ballad usually contained more strophes than did the lied and narrated an adventurous story. While it was frequently set to strophic music, other musical forms were occasionally employed. Koch observes that "The melody of the ballad, its character being determined by the content of the poem, is in neither a particular form nor a particular meter. Unlike the lied, in which each strophe of the text is set to repeated music, one has begun lately to compose the text throughout."[8] The practice of setting a strophic poem to through-composed music, although initially a controversial one, began to gain favor at the turn of the century. The new form permitted a closer, more flexible correlation between the changing poetic images of the strophes and the musical intensity of both the melody and accompaniment. In settings of exceptionally lengthy ballads, such as Bürger's *Lenore* of thirty-two strophes, in which a strophic form might become tediously repetitious, it had the additional advantage of allowing for greater musical variety.

In the generation following Koch, the lied was often defined as being not only a poetic genre but a musical one as well. One year after Goethe's death, the volumes of Herleßsohn's *Dammenkonversationslexikon* began to appear, where both forms of the word were entered. As a genre of poetry, the lied was like an ode; it was intended for singing in a simple style that expressed tender feelings. But under its second entry, the lied became a separate genre of music, although judging from the definition provided, its musical style seems to have changed little since the turn of the century.

> The lied . . . is the purest expression of our feelings in the simplest form; it speaks the language of truth in a charming way, and is echoed within our hearts. . . . The composer must set forth the most exuberant expressions of his imagination; . . . the singer must express in tones his innermost feelings, the secrets of his heart. The lied is the companion to German domesticity; the triumph of music in a circle of friendly souls. . . . In music the essential requirements of the lied concern the beauty and singability of the melody, natural but interesting harmonies, and an appropriate accompaniment that enhances the voice. Concerning the form of the lied, we have at last accepted in music the freedom of poetry; nevertheless the simple, basic form that we find in folk songs will always predominate.[9]

The author of this definition claims that Zelter and Reichardt were among the founders of the lied, and that the latter's melodies still sound like innocent nursery rhymes. By contrast, the works of Berger and Klein, he claims, are deep in poetic spirit, while among living composers, the songs of Loewe and Marschner are especially distinguished. As in Koch's definition, the Biedermeier ideals of simplicity and innocence seem to have been held as principal goals of the genre. As this definition, and others like it written toward the middle of the century, does not acknowledge the richness that Schubert had imparted to the genre, it appears that the discussion is based on works of the previous generation, or that it intentionally ignores songs in more complex forms.

There is in this definition an observation that is reaffirmed in many discussions of the lied to the present day. Recently it has been suggested that in the works of Schubert, the lied takes on such broad dimensions and so fully embraces the style of Romanticism that Schubert's lieder were in his own day considered by some to be beyond the acceptable limits of that genre.[10]

As one writer claimed in 1824, Schubert "does not write proper lieder, nor does he intend to . . . , but rather songs, sometimes so freely that one could possibly call them caprices or phantasies."[11] The older *volkstümliches Lied* (folk-like song), suitable for intimate domestic enjoyment, was gradually abandoned in favor of the more demanding and public style of the art song. After the death of Schubert it gradually became common for composers and publishers to distinguish in the titles of songs between *Lied*, *Gesang*, and later even *Gedicht*.[12]

Those songs designated as *Lied* often retain at least a few of the features associated with this genre from the beginning of the nineteenth century, and the term still seems to imply a simple, syllabic folksong style. These songs are often in strophic or modified-strophic forms; some are even based on folk poetry. As its name might imply, *Gesang* suggests a song in which attention is drawn to the melody (i.e., the voice) as the expressive vehicle for the poem. The poetry of these songs represents a variety of sorts, from the simple, direct, and regular to, more often, the profound; the musical forms likewise range from strophic to more complex patterns. In a similar manner, songs designated as *Gedicht* draw attention to the more sophisticated style of art poetry, something beyond the folk-like style appropriate to the *Lied*, and often require resourceful musical devices in their setting. While the terms continued to be used by composers, such as Richard Strauss, the musical and poetic distinctions between the three genres were often unclear by the end of the nineteenth century.

Throughout the nineteenth century the lied grew considerably in artistic sophistication, from the restrained, at times folk-like style of Zumsteeg and Reichardt to the more challenging operatic settings of Wolf, Rheinberger, and Zölner at the end of the century. During the same time the popularity of this genre increased remarkably as both a form of domestic enjoyment and as a genre for public concerts. Schumann expressed alarm in 1839 over the plethora of mediocre lieder on the commercial market; Wolf, nearly fifty years later, complained about the predominance of solo songs on public recital programs.[13] It is clear from such comments, and from numerous other written sources, that by the middle of the century the word *Lied* had begun to lose the specific connotations it had had in the earlier years of the century. One example of this change may suffice. Schumann's *Fünf Lieder*, op. 40 (1840), is based on four poems by Hans Christian Anderson and one poem translated from modern Greek by Chamisso. In musical style these songs contain few features one would regard as folk-like; their melodic phrases are occasionally imbalanced, their harmonies are moderately chromatic, and their forms are not strictly strophic. However, it was probably the style of poetry alone, which relies on folk-like images of innocence, reverence, and bucolic simplicity, that led Schumann and his publisher to adopt the word *Lied* for the title of these songs.

By the end of the nineteenth century, the word *Lied* assumed the meaning that it carries for many today: a solo song sung in German with keyboard accompaniment. In his *Musik-Lexikon* Hugo Riemann abandons the proscriptive definition of *Lied* found in earlier sources. His discussion of the genre, an account of its historical development, is careful to distinguish the "authentic" (eigentlich) style of the lied found in the older works from the style of more recent songs. He insists that the authentic lied is a strophic poem sung to strophic music in which a limited number of phrases alternate. A new style of the lied, he observes, began in the early nineteenth century with the poetic works of Goethe and the compositions of Schubert, from which emerged the songs of Mendelssohn, Schumann, Franz, Brahms, and others. Riemann complains that in the songs of the modern composers Liszt, Wolf, and Reger, the use of the voice in a declamatory rather than a melodic manner will inevitably lead to the demise of the genre.[14]

In recent times we have become accustomed to referring to German solo songs from the nineteenth and twentieth centuries as *Lieder* without formally distinguishing that genre of song, as it was defined early in the nineteenth century, from the many others such as ballad, romance, or *Gesang*. For example, the first song of this anthology, Zelter's "Nur wer die Sehnsucht kennt," is by early nineteenth-century standards technically not a *Lied* in either its poetic or musical forms; the tone of its single strophe is too serious, the form of its setting too complex. Zumsteeg's "Das Blümlein Wunderschön," its dramatic features notwithstanding, would probably have been more comfortably accepted as a *Lied* under Koch's definition.

Before the middle of the nineteenth century, the increasingly broad public acceptance of the lied was partly due to the accomplishments of the poets themselves. A new style of poetry had begun to emerge at the end of the eighteenth century in the works of Lessing, Schiller, Goethe, and others. Important to this style was the tone and atmospheric language that focused less on narrative events than on the feelings they engendered. It was probably this lyrical resonance, central to which were personal feelings and experiences, that made this poetry so appealing to the rapidly expanding German middle class and to a new generation of composers. At the turn of the century, these poems were widely available in a variety of sources, including *Taschenbücher*, literary almanacs, periodicals, and anthologies. After the second decade of the century, the works of Schiller and Goethe were available in collected editions. Just as it may be claimed that Beethoven had indirectly contributed to the sophistication of the keyboard sonata by expanding its dramatic capabilities, so also did these poets contribute directly to the expressive range of the lied by greatly elevating the artistic quality of its poetry.

Goethe and the Lied

Although Goethe never formally gathered his ideas on music into a codified theory, his letters and recorded conversations as well as his poetic and dramatic works contain insightful comments on music and its relationship to other arts.[15] Like many philosophers and poets of the nineteenth century, Goethe held music in very high regard, as something beyond mere entertainment, and his musical experiences often directly inspired his creative activity. He believed that music touched both the mind and heart of man, was capable of soothing the spirit, could build moral confidence, and could stimulate the powers of reason.

The impression that emerges from Goethe's many writings on the subject is that in Goethe's opinion music's advantage over other arts was also its flaw. Although music lacks an objective subject, and is therefore the most irrational of the arts, it is, according to the poet, capable of expressing deeply profound feelings and inarticulate thoughts in a more sensual way than any other art. In *Wilhelm Meisters Wanderjahre* Goethe wrote that "The value of art seems to be perhaps most eminent with music, because it has no subject that must be imputed. It is only form and content and elevates and ennobles all that it expresses."[16] Music was for Goethe, and for many of his early nineteenth-century contemporaries, a language of emotions transcendent of reason, even of the revelation of God, that was experienced as a play of forms in the imagination.[17] When once asked how much musicians were capable of imitating, he replied, "Nothing and everything. Nothing that we receive directly through the external senses; but everything that we feel inwardly through the intermediary of these senses. . . . The great and noble advantage of music is its ability to create a mood within us without using the common external means."[18] It was through music that man was permitted to enter the unfathomable world of feelings.

In Goethe's opinion purely instrumental music was, however, too imprecise to render its experience enduring, and only through song, i.e., texted music, whose meaning can be more accurately defined, could music appeal to both the mind and the spirit: "Melodies, progressions, and figures without words and sense seem to me to be similar to butterflies or beautifully colorful birds that flutter about in the air before our eyes, which we sometimes want to catch and keep; but those of the voice appear as a spirit raised to heaven who invites the better part of us to accompany him."[19] A subjective humanist, Goethe maintained that poetry could be rendered more expressive through the accompaniment of music, which intensifies its affective content. Asserting that the lied was complete only when it was set to music, Goethe actively encouraged musical settings of his poems, especially the "lieder" and "Gesellige Lieder," and even considered including music within his published collections.[20] In the poem "An Lina" he admonished, "Nur nicht lesen! immer singen! / Und ein jedes Blatt ist dein" ("Don't just read! sing always! / And every page is yours"), a thought that became especially appropriate to many nineteenth-century poets and musicians for whom music, not poetry, was preeminent.

Largely because of his reverence for folk song settings, Goethe preferred strophic settings of his lieder, in which the music, bound by the text and never independent of it, is derived from prosody and provides support for the poem. It was only through strophic settings, he argued, that poetic nuances could convincingly be projected and a unified impression dominate, since the repetition of stanzas placed the music in the background. The poems, Goethe contended, owed their inspiration to melody and converted naturally back into melody, so that elaborate musical accompaniment was unnecessarily distracting. In the case of the through-composed lied, Goethe felt that the distinctive musical treatment of strophes drew so much attention to poetic and musical details that the integrity of the poem was disrupted. Nevertheless, in performances he insisted that the singer slightly modify each strophe in tempo, dynamics, and intensity of inflection according to the poetic image.[21]

As might be expected of a poet, Goethe seems to have been less concerned with the quality of the voice that might sing his lieder than with the attention the singer should give to the interpretation of the poem. In fact, during the later years of the eighteenth century, the lied was a very popular musical genre (among certain circles perhaps the most popular), but was nearly always performed in private settings and sung by amateurs.[22] Once during an evening with Tomaschek, Goethe encouraged the composer to sing settings of his poems, contending that composers knew better how to enliven a lied than did trained singers. He added, "the full effect of the *Lied* depends less on the beauty of the voice than on the emphasis given appropriately to specific passages."[23]

In their meter and language, many of Goethe's poems strongly suggest inherently musical properties. Through assonance and onomatopoeia some verses, such as "Rastlose Liebe," even sound musical when read aloud. It is even possible that many of his poems, especially those that have been set so frequently to music, were written under the influence of song. For example, Goethe was inspired to write the poem "Nahe des Geliebten" (in this anthology set by Tomaschek [3] and Hiller [11]) by a melody which Zelter had written to set a poem of that title by Friederike Brun.[24] In the novel *Wilhelm Meister* Goethe gave the protagonist a confession that has been interpreted by some as autobiographical: "I am denied a pleasant voice by nature . . . but it seems to me often that a hidden spirit whispers something rhythmical to me, so that as I walk I always move to it in rhythm, and simultaneously seem to hear faint sounds, the accompaniment of some song which somehow pleasantly suggests itself to me."[25] One might suggest that the strongly melodic and rhythmic features of Goethe's verses have been a significant factor in their becoming so popular among composers.

During Goethe's time it was suggested by musicians that the melodies associated with folk poems might be adopted as models of a new style of song, just as it was suggested that the poems themselves could rejuvenate modern poetry. In a book that was widely read, C. F. D. Schubart, a composer and poet both, recommended that "one should study our divine folk melodies, whose influences have already been felt for over a century; only then will one compose a lied that our people will accept."[26] Many of Goethe's most famous verses were written in a style drawn from folk poetry. J. W. Smeed has pointed out that Goethe's *Heidenröslein* was written in direct imitation of a familiar song, and the famous *Erlkönig* (Klein [8]) was inspired by a translated version of a Danish folk ballad. Other poems, such as *Jägers Abendlied*, and *Mailied* (here set by Pfitzner [19]), use simple forms and images common to folk poems, but are written in more eloquent tones.[27] In *Mailied*, for example, as in many poems of this type, the subject's initial delight in a natural scene, here the morning landscape, is eventually mixed with his ecstatic love for a *Mädchen*. Later the newness of the dawn is made analogous to the awakening of his love. As the skylark depends upon the air in which it flies to sing its songs, so also does the poet gain through his beloved the joy and courage to create new poems.

Others of Goethe's poems combine the form and details of folk style with more refined and elevated sentiments. In such works as *Erlkönig, Der Fischer,* and *König in Thule* (given here as [8], [7], and [9] respectively) the expressive range of the folk model is broadened to allow for deeper and more subtle expression. For example, the meaning of *König in Thule* can be interpreted on more than just one level. There is, of course, the obvious meaning of the narrative, wherein the king throws his cup into the sea and dies. But a more satisfying understanding of the poem, implied by its first strophe, might be derived by interpreting the goblet symbolically: that which was bequeathed to the king by his dying wife he refuses to relinquish and dies upon parting with it. The goblet becomes a symbol of his wife's love from which he metaphorically drinks each evening to sustain his soul. This love is his, his alone, and so as he dies and returns to dust, he can only return it to nature's elements. To most composers who have set this poem, it was surely the deeper implications of the story that suggested a style of musical setting more poignant than merely a tuneful drinking song, one more demanding of the accompaniment and more evocative in its melody.

For some of Goethe's poems the context in which they first appeared may also influence their musical setting on yet another level. This may be the case with [1], [6], [8], [9 (18)], [13], and [16] of this anthology, where the poems first appeared as part of larger dramas, although most were later published also in collections of poetry. *König in Thule*, for example, was written for *Faust*, where it is sung by Margaret as she prepares for bed. She had met Faust earlier that day and, although she had rebuffed him, she now finds herself drawn to him. When interpreted within the context of the drama, the poem suggests a symbolic story of enduring love: Margaret sees Faust as the king of the poem, steadfast in his love for his bride. Finishing the song, she opens her wardrobe and discovers a casket of jewels that Faust had hidden. The jewels are a symbol of Faust's love, just as the golden goblet of the song was a symbol to the King of Thule.

The Songs

From the beginning of the nineteenth century, the *Lieder* genre was represented by a large diversity of musical styles and forms, so that it is misleading to speak loosely of a singular song form or even of a finite collection of formal stereotypes. Songs have always been cast in as great a variety of structures and styles as the poems themselves. In addition to the simple strophic form of the *volkstümliches Lied*, there are rounded binary and ternary forms as well as many other far more complex structures (such as rondo and through-composed forms, and operatic-like formulas of recitative and arias). There are often great differences in the forms of songs within a single collection or song cycle. None of the fifteen lieder in the cycle *Die schöne Magelone* by Brahms, for example, is in the same form, and none of these songs conform strictly to familiar strophic or ternary designs. But discussions of lieder must account not only for the structure of songs but also for the diversity of their basic types. For in addition to the familiar style of the lied as a song, we also encounter declamatory lieder, dialogue ballads, and even songs in styles resembling operatic scenes.

The songs of this anthology represent a large variety of these musical structures, from the fairly simple to the complex, and although we may use the same terms to describe many of them, each is unique and none corresponds literally to the restrictive definitions of the lied cited above. The distinction between strophic and through-composed songs may not have been as apparent to listeners at the beginning of the nineteenth century as it seems to us today. The verses of strophic songs may have been performed with slight variations to accommodate different moods of the text, and in many strophic songs the final verse was altered in order to bring the work to a convincing close. For example, while the setting of "Als ich still und ruhig spann" by Ries (*Die Spinnerin* [5]) appears to be a simple strophic form, comparison with Goethe's poem reveals that, except for the last, each strophe of music contains not one but two stanzas of poetry. Zelter's *Sehnsucht* [1], by contrast, makes a modified strophic form (A–A') of a single stanza of poetry by dividing its twelve lines into two equal parts. In the modified strophic form of Spohr's *Mignons Lied* [6], the keyboard accompaniment is varied in each of the three strophes; while each begins with and ends with similar melodic phrases, the strophes are different in the central periods. The form of this song is in its details appreciably different from the song by Hiller *Nähe des Geliebten* [11], which, lacking more appropriate terminology, we must also describe as modified strophic. Busoni's *Lied des Mephistopheles* [18] is, likewise, a modified strophic form in which each stanza of poetry corresponds to one section of music, but although each musical section begins similarly, all continue in different ways. The central verses in Klein's setting of "Wer reitet so spät" (*Erlkönig* [8]), a strophic poem, are gathered in pairs and are set in modified strophic fashion. Contrarily, some through-composed lieder contain large sections of music that are repeated. The forms of the songs by Pfitzner [19], Medtner [21], and Schoeck [22] are all through-composed, yet each treats the individual poetic stanzas in unique musical ways.

The two songs by Tomaschek are each similar in general formal shape. Although folk-like in language and sentiment, "Ein Veilchen auf der Wiese stand" (*Das Veilchen* [4]) is a challenging poem for any composer, as its three stanzas are made up of an odd number of lines (seven) which do not all contain the same number of stresses. Tomaschek's ternary setting of this deceptively complex poem contributes to its irregularity by initiating the final reprise only after two lines of the final verse. In *Nähe des Geliebten* [3] Tomaschek seems less at ease in setting a strophic poem with lines of seven stresses; in this poem, the poetic phrases do not correspond to the poetic lines.

The setting of "O! gib vom weichen Pfüle" by Rheinberger (*Nachtgesang* [15]), also a modified strophic example, uses two stanzas of poetry in each musical strophe. Marschner's *Der König von Thule* [9] is a ternary design in which each of the three parts (A–A'–A") is a double period containing two stanzas of poetry. *Wonne der Wehmut* by Robert Franz [12] is set to a poem only one strophe in length, and its phrases are arranged as an arch form, ABA, while Rubinstein's *Clärchens Lied* [13], also set to a poem only one strophe long, is through-composed. The poem "Laßt mich nur auf meinem Sattel gelten!" comprises two strophes, but it is set by Bülow (*Freisinn* [14]) as a ternary form (ABA') in which the first strophe is repeated. The poem "Verfliesset, vielgeliebte Lieder," two verses in length, is arranged by Mendelssohn (*Am Flusse* [17]) in a rounded binary form (ABA') in which the last two lines of poetry are set to a variation of the opening phrase. Mendelssohn's *Wer sich der Einsamkeit ergibt* [16] is cast as a repeated binary form, ABAB. Finally, the form of Wetzel's *An den Mond* [20] is an imbalanced form in three parts, ABA', in which the first contains three strophes of poetry, the second has four (arranged as two plus two), and the third has two.

The setting of "Ich Kenn' ein Blümlein Wunderschön" by Zumsteeg (*Das Blümlein Wunderschön* [2]) requires special comment. The poem is an example of a dialogue ballad in which a conversation is described or suggested. In the case of Goethe's "Blümlein" the characters of the drama are specifically identified in the poem. More often, however, their identity is not specified but is made clear within the context of the poem, as in "Hat der alte Hexenmeister" (*Der Zauberlehrling* [10]) or "Wer reitet so spät" (*Erlkönig* [8]). The representation of characters can also be seen in poems that are not strictly narrative ballads, as in the famous "Der

Tod und das Mädchen" by Claudius. The suspicion is strong that in certain cases, especially where the separate dramatic parts are clearly marked (for example, in Reichardt's *Der Müllerin Reue*), these songs may have been performed in domestic settings as small dramas, a *Liederspiel*, in which the parts were enacted by different voices.[28] A very popular genre during the early years of the nineteenth century, the larger dramatic settings such as Zumsteeg's seem to have fallen out of favor later in the century.

Two songs of the anthology, Hauptmann's *Der Fischer* [7] and Mendelssohn's *Am Flusse* [17], represent a genre that was quite popular during the nineteenth century, but one that has not as yet received adequate scholarly attention. This is the genre of the ensemble lied, that is, a song accompanied by keyboard and one or more instruments. The genre stands midway between the solo keyboard lied and the orchestral lied that began to emerge around the middle of the nineteenth century. Certain notable examples of this genre will be familiar to many readers, such as Schubert's *Der Hirt auf dem Felsen*, D. 965 (for voice, piano, and clarinet), his *Auf dem Strom*, D. 943 (for voice, piano, and French horn), and Beethoven's folk song settings WoO 152–55 and 157–58 (for voice, piano, violin, and violoncello). But many other less well-known instrumental lieder deserve serious study. For example, the songs from Spohr's *Sechs Gesänge*, op. 154 (for baritone, violin, and piano) or his *Sechs deutsche Lieder*, op. 103 (for voice and piano with obbligato clarinet) are excellent examples of this genre. In many of these works the part for the additional instrument was derived from either the keyboard or the voice, its function being to reinforce and embellish these other parts. In the two songs by Hauptmann and Mendelssohn, however, the accompanying instrument is independent of the voice and keyboard and participates equally in the setting as a third partner. Although the accompaniment in such lieder commonly involves keyboard and only one other instrument (frequently violin), there are also songs that require larger instrumental forces. In some songs scored for chamber ensemble the keyboard is eliminated, such as in Wolf's *Harfenspieler II* (for five solo winds and strings) and his *Auf ein altes Bild* (for two oboes, two clarinets, and two bassoons).[29]

Composers and Musical Sources

[1] Born in Berlin, Carl Friedrich Zelter (1758–1832) became one of that city's most distinguished musicians throughout its history. After 1774 he studied violin and within four years was able to assist in performances by local orchestras. With Carl Fasch, who established the Berlin Singakademie, he studied composition, and his own works began to be performed publicly after 1782. After taking over direction of the Singakademie in 1800, Zelter turned the chorus into one of Germany's most renowned organizations in the rediscovery of older music. He became Professor of Music at the Berlin Academy of Fine Arts in 1809, where his students included Felix Mendelssohn, Loewe, and Meyerbeer.

Zelter wrote more than 200 lieder, which, along with those of his contemporary Reichardt, were important in the formation of the musical style known as the second Berlin school. From 1796 to his death, Zelter set seventy-five poems by Goethe. When his songs were brought to Goethe's attention in 1798, the poet remarked that Zelter's lieder were "an absolute reproduction of the poetic intentions" of his verses. After 1799 Goethe and Zelter corresponded frequently, and their published letters, a testament of their sincere friendship, contain numerous discussions of music.[30]

Zelter's setting of "Nur wer die Sehnsucht kennt" presented here is one of three songs he wrote on this text, one of which was published in Friedlaender's *Gedichte von Goethe in Kompositionen seiner Zeitgenossen*. When compared to his other settings of this poem, this version is more adventurous in its harmonies (avoiding a convincing cadence on the tonic until the end of the piece) and more melodically chromatic.

The source for this edition of Zelter's *Sehnsucht* ("Nur wer die Sehnsucht kennt") is the first edition (1827): Sechs | Deutsche Lieder | für die Altstimme | mit Begleitung des Pianoforte | in Musik gesetzt | von | C. F. Zelter | Berlin bei T. Trautwein, plate number 200. The copy consulted is in the Library of Congress, Music Division, Washington, D.C.

[2] Born in 1760, Johann Rudolf Zumsteeg (1760–1802) established an impressive reputation as a cellist, composer, and conductor in the south German city of Stuttgart, where he resided nearly all his life. He was a close friend of the poet Friedrich von Schiller. As a youth Zumsteeg received a thorough musical education at a military academy, his father being in the service of duke Carl Eugen. After 1781 he was solo cellist in the Stuttgart court orchestra and began to compose operas, incidental music for plays, and cantatas for the court. Ten years later he became director of German music at the court theater and in 1793 was promoted to court *Konzertmeister*. In this position he supported performances of dramatic works by Mozart and achieved success with his own opera *Die Geisterinsel*. Before his death in 1802 he composed several operas, singspiels, incidental music, secular and sacred cantatas, songs, and numerous chamber and orchestral works, including ten concertos for violoncello.

The lieder of Zumsteeg, about 300 altogether, form an important link between the north German style of Zelter and Reichardt and the art songs of Schubert, who was in several of his songs directly influenced by Zumsteeg's setting of the same texts. Zumsteeg's ballads and lieder, published after 1791, were highly regarded by his contemporaries for their sensitive prosody. They were cast in a large variety of forms—strophic, through-composed, and other song forms—and in styles of declamation including arioso, recitative, and folk-like lyricism. Among the 168 lieder published in the seven volumes of *Kleine Balladen und Lieder* between 1800 and 1805, only six are set to poems by Goethe.[31]

Das Blümlein Wunderschön is an example of the dialogue ballad, a cantata-like song the text to which involves characters of a drama, and which may actually have been performed by more than one singer, as a *Liederspiel*. The genre was especially popular during the Biedermeier period, a time of domestic sentimentality in the styles of some artists during the first third of the nineteenth century, but is found less frequently afterward.

The source for this edition of Zumsteeg's *Das Blümlein Wunderschön* ("Ich kenn' ein Blümlein Wunderschön") is the first edition (1801): Kleine | Balladen und Lieder | mit Klavierbegleitung | von | J. R. Zumsteeg | Dritter Heft | Bey Breitkopf und Härtel in Leipzig, plate number 1414. The copy consulted is in the Newberry Library, Chicago, IL.

[3] Educated in mathematics, philosophy, and law, the Bohemian composer Wenzel Johann Tomaschek (1774–1850) was largely a self-taught musician who achieved distinction, especially in Prague (where he lived most of his life), as a pianist, organist, teacher, and composer. Among his 114 compositions with opus numbers are sacred and secular choral works, operas, and other dramatic settings, including *Gretchen aus Goethes Faust*, op. 102 (for voice and orchestra), and *Szene aus Goethes Faust*, op. 103 (for soloists, chorus, and orchestra).[32] However, Tomaschek is known primarily for his lyrical keyboard works, which contributed to the emergence of the new forms of keyboard character pieces. These works include seven sets of six eclogues, fifteen rhapsodies, three *ditrambi*, and several sets of variations. His works were publicly acclaimed by Berlioz, Schumann, and Wagner. The composer Johann Vorisek and the prominent Viennese music critic Eduard Hanslick were two of Tomaschek's many students.

Tomaschek wrote a large number of lieder, over two-thirds of which are settings of German poets, especially Goethe, Heine, Schiller, and Gellert. In 1815 he completed nine volumes of *Gedichte von Goethe*, opp. 53–61, containing thirty-four solo songs, three duets, and four trios. Along with Zelter and Reichardt, Tomaschek was one of a small number of composers acquainted with Goethe, and he took seriously the task of setting large numbers of Goethe's poems. When Tomaschek sent a collection of his settings to Goethe in 1818, the two began to correspond and eventually met in 1822. Goethe proclaimed that he preferred Tomaschek's setting of his poem "Kennst du das Land?" over those by Beethoven and Spohr.[33]

It seems unlikely that Goethe would have expressed such enthusiasm for Tomaschek's *Nähe des Geliebten* or *Das Veilchen*, for in both of these songs, the composer ignored the strophic form of the poems in favor of a through-composed setting of the verses. Unlike Schubert, who cast *Nähe des Geliebten* as a strophic song, Tomaschek gave special emphasis in his setting to the anxious sentiments of verses two and three. The second verse moves briefly to C minor for the phrase "in tiefer Nacht," and throughout the two inner verses the lower part of the accompaniment is more active in rhythm. The independence of the accompaniment from the voice, both in rhythm and melody, is for its time noteworthy. In the setting of the three verses of *Das Veilchen*, Tomaschek adopted a similarly arched form, in which the harmonies of the inner verse move away from the tonic (especially with the bold chords at the end of this verse), and the third verse returns initially to the opening phrase, this time in the tonic minor.

The source for this edition of Tomaschek's *Nähe des Geliebten* ("Ich denke dein") is the first edition (1815): Nähe des Geliebten: Gedichte von Goethe | für den Gesang | mit Begleitung des Piano = forte | gesetzt von | Wenzel J. Tomáschek, Tonsetzer bey Herrn Georg Grafen von Buguoy. | Eigenthum des Verlegers | Prag bei Marco Berra. [op. 53, no. 1], plate number 501. The copy consulted is in the University of California, Berkeley, Music Library, Berkeley, CA.

[4] The source for this edition of Tomaschek's *Das Veilchen* ("Ein Veilchen auf der Wiese stand") is the first edition (1815): Gedichte von Goethe | für den Gesang | mit Begleitung des Piano = forte | gesetzt von | Wenzel J. Tomáschek, Tonsetzer bey Herrn Georg Grafen von Buguoy. | Eigenthum des Verlegers | Prag bei Marco Berra. [op. 57, no. 1], plate number 500. The copy consulted is in the University of California, Berkeley, Music Library, Berkeley, CA.

[5] Ferdinand Ries (1784–1838) was the son of a violinist from whom he learned piano and violin at an early age. His most notable teacher was Ludwig van Beethoven. Beethoven had studied piano and composition with Ries's father in Bonn and in Vienna. It was through Beethoven that Ries was introduced to the wealthy society of Vienna, including Prince Lichnowsky. He made an acclaimed debut as Beethoven's pupil in 1804, playing Beethoven's Piano Concerto in C minor. The years 1807 and 1808 were spent in Paris and Vienna respectively, but they brought Ries little public recognition. Then in 1809 Ries embarked on a series of concert tours that were very successful throughout northern Europe for the next four years. At the conclusion of this period he arrived in London, where he was introduced to the Philharmonic Concerts by J. P. Salomon, and where he resided from 1813 to 1824. In London he built a reputation as one of the finest pianists and teachers of his day. Although Beethoven criticized Ries's compositions as being merely imitations of his own, Ries steadfastly spoke out in support of him. Ries was able to retire in 1824 to Frankfurt am Main, and before his death, he was active on behalf of the Lower Rhine Music Festivals.

A prolific composer in nearly all genres, Ries published 186 compositions, including operas, several symphonies, overtures, and chamber works, many involving piano. However, his reputation was based largely on his works for keyboard, which include fourteen sonatas, many rondos, marches, fantasies, and numerous collections of variations. Although the style of certain of his keyboard works is formally and harmonically advanced, his fifty-four songs, written throughout his career, are largely in a conservative, folk-like style. His setting of

Die Spinnerin, typical of this style, is reminiscent of the style of Reichardt. All songs of the *Sechs Lieder,* op. 32, are based on texts by Goethe.

The source for this edition of Ries's *Die Spinnerin* ("Als ich still und ruhig spann") is the first edition (1811?): Sechs Lieder | mit | Begleitung des Pianoforte | in Musik gesetzt | von | Ferd: Ries. | 36s Werk. | Fünfte Samt: - der Gesangst: | Hamburg | Bey Johann August Böhme. Number 5. The copy consulted is in the Gesellschaft der Musikfreunde, Vienna, Austria.

[6] Born into a musical family, Louis Spohr (1784–1859) was as a child afforded frequent contact with a wide variety of chamber music, opera, and song. While still very young he began to compose music (largely works for the violin) and rapidly developed his talent as a violinist virtuoso, making his first solo tour of Europe in 1804. His first permanent position was in Gotha, where he resided for seven years as concert master in the ducal orchestra. While director of the orchestra at the Theater an der Wien, Vienna, from 1813 to 1815, Spohr completed a two-act opera on *Faust* (the libretto was not drawn from Goethe's drama), which premiered in Prague in 1816 under the direction of Carl Maria von Weber. In Frankfurt as director of the opera from 1817 to 1819, he produced one of his most successful operas, *Zemire und Azor*. From 1822 until his retirement in 1857, Spohr resided in Kassel as kapellmeister to the court, responsible for performances of instrumental music and of opera. He continued to perform as a violinist throughout Europe, but also strengthened his reputation as a composer with successful performances of works in large genres, notably the opera *Jessonda* (1823) and the oratorio *Die letzten Dinge* (1826). His efforts on behalf of the music of Bach and Wagner were influential.

Spohr was one of Germany's most successful composers and virtuosi in the period between Haydn and Wagner. A prodigious composer in all genres, he published ten volumes of lieder between 1810 and 1857 containing over 90 songs, many of which became very popular during his life. The volumes published as opp. 25 and 37 contain some of the earliest settings of Goethe's poetry, including *Gretchen* and *Mignon's Lied*, by a composer outside the poet's immediate circle.

Spohr's setting of "Kennst du das Land" (*Mignon's Lied*) is unique among his songs. Perhaps in an attempt to set comfortably the natural accents of the poem, he calls for changes in meter with uncharacteristic frequency, and in so doing gives his setting a compelling sense of urgency that is not found in other settings of this poem before Hugo Wolf's. The broad pace with which the questions at the beginning of the first and third strophes are declaimed, for example, and the sensitive prosody throughout are bold strokes for lieder of this period.

The source for this edition of Spohr's *Mignons Lied* ("Kennst du das Land?") is the first edition 1816: Sechs Deutsche Lieder | mit Begleitung des Pianoforte | in Musik gesetzt | und | Ihrer durchlaucht der regierenden Frau | Fürstin von Carolath Schönaich | ehrfurchtsvoll zugeeignet | von . Louis Spohr. | Zweite Sammlung Lieder | 37st Werk . . . | Leipzig | im Bureau de Musique von C. F. Peters | (Diese Lieder sind auch mit Begleitung der Guitarre zu haben.) No. 1, plate number 1270. Copy in Newberry Library, Chicago, IL.

[7] Moritz Hauptmann (1792–1868) is known today primarily as a theorist of great musical insight, the author of *Die Natur der Harmonik und Metrik* (1853) and *Die Lehre von der Harmonik* (1868). He was born in Dresden in 1792, studied violin and composition with Spohr, and in 1812 moved to Vienna to play in Spohr's orchestra at the Theater an der Wien. Following an appointment in Dresden (1820–22), Hauptmann moved to Kassel, again to play violin in the court orchestra under Spohr. He remained in that position for the next twenty years, during which time he became recognized as both a theorist and a composer.

He moved to Leipzig in 1842 as director of the Thomasschule, where in the following year he became instructor of theory and composition at the new Leipzig Conservatory. His pupils included Joseph Joachim and Hans von Bülow. During the year 1843 he served as editor of the *Allgemeine musikalische Zeitung*. In 1850 Hauptmann was one of the principal founders of the Bach Gesellschaft; he edited the first three volumes of the Bach edition sponsored by that society, and he served as president of the society until his death.

For his own style of composition, Hauptmann held as models the works of Spohr, Felix Mendelssohn, and Schumann. He wrote a large number of works, the majority for voices, including two masses, sixteen motets, and two operas. His choral works found broad popularity by the middle of the century. Among all his works, he himself treasured his lieder the most, for which he held the folk song as the ideal. Twenty of his songs are set to the poetry of Goethe. Hauptmann may have been inspired to write ensemble lieder, such as *Der Fischer*, through his contact with works in that genre by his teacher, Louis Spohr. Hauptmann freely treats the strophic poem of *Der Fischer* in the musical form of ABCA', in which the first line of the second strophe is set as an extension of the first verse.

The source for this edition of Hauptmann's *Der Fischer* ("Das Wasser rauscht' ") is the first edition (1843): Drei Lieder | für eine Singstimme | mit | Pianoforte-und Violin-Begleitung | componirt und | Herrn Professor Dr. E. A. Carus | freundschaftlich zugeeignet | von | M Hauptmann | op. 31 | . . . Leipzig | im Bureau de Musique von C. F. Peters. [No. 3], plate number 2902. Copy in the Staatsbibliothek, Preußischer Kulturbesitz, Berlin, Germany.

[8] Before traveling to Paris in 1812 to study briefly with Cherubini, Bernhard Klein (1793–1832) learned his art largely autodidactically in Cologne. Upon his return from Paris, Klein accepted a position in Cologne as music director of the city's amateur concerts and of the large Cathedral, where his sacred music was well received. From 1818 until his death, Klein resided in Berlin and earned a reputation, especially in northern Germany,

through his compositions and his direction of the Liedertafel. After 1820, he became instructor of sacred music, thoroughbass, and counterpoint at the Royal Institute for Church Music. He studied music briefly with Zelter, but their relationship turned bitter and was never reconciled.

Although he composed in all genres, including operas and chamber music, Klein was most successful with his sacred vocal music and his lieder. Along with Ludwig Berger and Felix Mendelssohn, Klein was a significant force in the "Third Berlin School" of song composition. His works in this genre, generally simple, yet very expressive in their style, were widely known and were admired by Robert Schumann. Among his numerous songs are several collections of settings of texts by Goethe, including *Neun Lieder von Goethe,* op. 15 (1827) and *Vier Gedichte von Goethe,* op. 41 (1832).

Klein's setting of *Der Erlkönig* is not as insistent on the suggestive motoric rhythm in the accompaniment at the opening of the song as are Reichardt's, Schubert's, or even Loewe's settings of the same poem. Klein's ghostly monotone portrayal of the character of Erlkönig, however, bears a strong resemblance to Reichardt's setting of the poem.

The source for this edition of Klein's *Der Erlkönig* ("Wer reitet so spät") is the first edition (1827): Der Erlkönig | Ein Gedicht von Goethe | Mit Begleitung | des | Pianoforte | In Musik gesetzt | von | Bern. Klein. | Bonn und Cölln bey N. Simrock. Plate number 1147. Copy in Yale University Library, New Haven, CT.

[9] Before entering Leipzig University in 1813 as a student of jurisprudence, Heinrich August Marschner (1795–1861) had already composed a number of lieder and music for a ballet. Upon the encouragement of the influential music critic Johann Rochlitz, Marschner directed his studies to music. In 1816 Marschner was invited to Pressburg as music instructor in the employment of Count Zichy, where he gained notice as a pianist, composer, and pedagogue.

The success of Marschner's operas drew the attention of Carl Maria von Weber in Dresden, who performed his works and invited him to that court in 1821. Two years later Marschner was named codirector of the court opera with Weber and became kapellmeister of the Leipzig theater after the latter's death in 1826. The premieres of two of his operas in Leipzig, *Der Vampyr* (1828) and *Der Templer und die Jüdin* (1829), brought him widespread acclaim in Europe that was reaffirmed in 1833 by the success of *Hans Heiling.* From 1831 until his retirement in 1859, he resided in Hanover as kapellmeister to the court.

During his lifetime Marschner's public fame rested largely on the success of a few of his thirteen operas, which are important works in that genre during the period between Weber and Wagner. Throughout his career, he wrote over 420 lieder, many of which, especially the ballads, continued to be performed as *Hausmusik* for many years after his death. Marschner's *Der König von Thule* is sensitive to the prevailingly pensive mood of the play at the point when the poem is sung by Gretchen. The song is set as a modified strophic form in which each musical phrase contains a verse of poetry. Minor changes in either the voice or the accompaniment of individual phrases accommodate the various images of the poem, as in measures 36–40, where the king is heralded by the accompaniment.

The source for this edition of Marschner's *Der König von Thule* ("Es war ein König in Thule") is the first edition (1852): Herrn | Joseph Staudigl | K. K. Kammersänger in Wien. | Vier | Gesänge | für | eine Baritonstimme | mit Begleitung des Pianoforte | componirt von | Heinrich Marschner | op. 160 . . . Leipzig bei Friedrich Hofmeister. No. 1, plate number 4611. Copy in Staatsbibliothek, Preußischer Kulturbesitz, Berlin, Germany.

[10] As both singer and composer, Carl Loewe (1796–1869) was one of the most popular musicians during the second third of the nineteenth century. After receiving early instruction in piano, Loewe moved to Halle in 1809 to become a pupil of the famous theorist Daniel Gottlob Türk. There, as a member of the choral society, he so impressed the king of Westphalia with the beauty of his voice that he was given a generous annuity until 1813 to support his studies in music.

Upon the death of Türk in 1813, Loewe served for three years as organist at the church of St. Mark before taking up the study of theology at the university. Drawing attention as a promising composer, he made the acquaintance of Hummel, Weber, and, in 1820, Goethe. Upon his return from a brief musical tour of Germany in 1819 and 1820, he received an appointment as music director at the gymnasium in Stettin, a position he held for the rest of his life.

With the security of his position assured, Loewe turned more seriously to composition and in the following years completed numerous works in many genres. He received international recognition with successful performances in Berlin of the oratorio *Die Zerstörung Jerusalems* (1832) and the opera *Die drei Wünsche* (1834). As a singer he made several recital tours throughout Europe, with such acclaim that he was referred to as "the north German Schubert."[34]

Between 1824 and 1869 Loewe published 139 works in various genres with opus numbers, and twenty-six others without opus numbers. Known especially for his impressive settings of narrative ballads, Loewe published over 100 volumes of solo songs, many based on texts by German romantic poets, including thirty-two songs on poetry by Goethe. Loewe's songs were published in Leipzig between 1899 and 1904 in a complete edition, *Carl Loewes Werke: Gesamtausgabe der Balladen, Legenden, Lieder und Gesänge.* His *Drei Balladen,* op. 1, contains a setting of Goethe's *Erlkönig.* Goethe's poem on the legend of the sorcerer's apprentice, *Der Zauberlehrling,* was set by Loewe in 1830 as a ballad of virtuosic display for both voice and keyboard. Although the song gives the initial impression of being through-composed, closer study reveals its modified strophic form, with a refrain in D-flat after each strophe.

The source for this edition of Loewe's *Der Zauberlehrling* ("Hat der alte Hexenmeister") is the first edition (1832): Drei Balladen | (Das Hochzeitlied, der Zauberlehrling, | die wandelnde Glocke.) | von | Goethe | für eine Singstimme mit Begleitung | des Pianoforte | componirt | von | C. Loewe | . . . Op. 20 | . . . Berlin | in der Schlesinger'schen Buch' und Musikhandlung. No. 3, plate number 1755. Copy in Yale University Library, New Haven, CT.

[11] At an early age Ferdinand Hiller (1811–85) attracted the attention of many of the leading musicians of his day with his precocious piano playing. At the suggestions of Moscheles and Spohr, he moved from Frankfurt to Weimar in 1825 to study with J. N. Hummel. There he came in close association with Goethe, at whose home he occasionally played. Later, in 1883, Hiller was to publish an account of these experiences in his book *Goethes musikalisches Leben*.

On a journey with Hummel in 1827 to Vienna, Hiller met Schubert and Beethoven. For the next seven years, he lived in Paris, giving concerts and establishing a broad reputation as teacher and composer. He was accepted by prominent musicians, including Berlioz, Chopin, and Liszt (with whom he became close friends), and the poets Heine and Hugo.

For fourteen years after leaving Paris in 1836, Hiller lived in Italy and Germany, including three years in Dresden, where he enjoyed his association with Schumann and Wagner. After 1850 he lived in Cologne as that city's kapellmeister, he toured occasionally as a pianist, and he developed a reputation as an astute musical journalist.

Although known primarily as an excellent pianist, teacher, and conductor, Hiller also enjoyed a modest reputation as a composer. The performance of his oratorio *Die Zerstörung Jerusalems* in Leipzig, 1840, was one of his greatest successes. He published over thirty small collections of solo songs on both sacred and secular texts, two lieder cycles, and *Volksthümliche Lieder*. His *Gesang der Geister über dem Wassern*, op. 36, for chorus and orchestra, is based on a text by Goethe. In the deeply expressive atmosphere it creates and its colorful harmonies, Hiller's *Nähe des Geliebten* seems to derive its inspiration from the model of Schumann. The composer accommodates the challenging irregularity of the poetic lines by alternating seven-bar and six-bar phrases (in the first three strophes only) in the voice that are filled out by the accompaniment to make eight-bar phrases.

The source for this edition of Hiller's *Nähe des Geliebten* ("Ich denke dein") is an early print (not the first edition), ca. 1870: Lieder | fur eine Altstimme | mit Begleitung des Pianoforte | von | Ferdinand Hiller. Divided title page, with contents of op. 111 on the left, and that of op. 129 on the right. Heft 1 . . . No. 1. Nähe des Geliebten . . . Bremen bei Aug. Fr. Cranz. Copy in Boston Public Library, Boston, MA.

[12] The early musical education of the young Robert Franz (1815–92) was acquired through the study of works by Bach, Handel, and contemporary romantic masters. His professional career began in 1841 with his appointment as organist (and the following year as director of the choir) at Halle's Ulrichskirche. Following the publication of his *Zwölf Gesänge,* op. 1, in 1843, which drew favorable comments from, among others, Robert Schumann, his reputation as a composer of *Gesänge* broadened. His works were respected by some of the most progressive musicians of his day, including Joachim and Liszt, who published an extended assessment of Franz in 1872. Because of progressive deafness, Franz was forced to give up his musical career early; he published his last set of songs, op. 52, in 1884.

Franz must be considered one of the central figures in the history of the nineteenth-century lied. He wrote close to 350 songs, nearly one-fourth set to poems by Heine, fifty-one to poems by Franz's friend Osterwald, and many others to the romantic poets Eichendorff and Mörike; however, there are only eight songs on the poetry of Goethe. His models in this genre were the songs of Schubert and Schumann, although he also admitted to studying old German folk songs, some of which he set to modern lyrics. The style of his *Wonne der Wehmut*, with its persistent rhythm and colorful harmonies (especially in mm. 18ff) is evidence of his fondness for Schumann. Although the song begins in the key of B-flat minor, the first and second phrases cadence on the dominant F (mm. 9 and 16), as does the final cadence of the song. The song's open phrases seem to support the subject of the poem, love's pain, and may also reflect the composer's attempt to join this song to the second one of the collection in op. 33, "Gegenwart," which is in B-flat major and begins on its dominant, and which announces the arrival of the beloved.

The source for this edition of Franz's *Wonne der Wehmut* ("Trocknet nicht") is the first edition (1861): Sechs Lieder | von | Goethe | für eine Singstimme | mit Begleitung des Pianoforte | componirt | von | Robert Franz | op. 33 . . . Leipzig: F. Whistling. No. 1, plate number 900 (901). Copy in Newberry Library, Chicago, IL.

[13] A child virtuoso, Anton Rubinstein (1829–94) gave his first public concert as a pianist at the age of nine. He was then taken on a tour of the major European cities, meeting heads of state and such prominent musicians as Chopin and Liszt. After 1844 Rubinstein spent two years studying composition in Berlin and two years as an impoverished teacher in Vienna. His misfortune turned when, upon his return to Russia in 1849, he was given permanent residence in a palace of the tsar's sister-in-law. As a result of several very successful European tours after 1854, Rubinstein gradually gained a reputation as one of the greatest pianists of his day. Taking an interest in Russian musical education, he helped establish the Russian Musical Society in 1859 and the St. Petersburg Conservatory three years later, which he directed until 1867 (and again after 1887).

As a composer, pedagogue, and essayist, Rubinstein had an enormous influence on the musical culture of Russia in the second half of the nineteenth century. He wrote a large number of works in many genres, although few remain in the repertoire today. His early symphonies and piano concerti were among the first Russian works in these genres.[35] Of his 160 lieder, nearly sixty are settings of German poets, including Heine and Goethe, and others are set to Russian (e.g., Tolstoy), and French (e.g., Hugo) poets. His brief setting of *Clärchens Lied* is typical of Rubinstein's harmonic style. Here he suggests the poem's exuberance by disjunct motion and rapid declamation in the voice, by avoiding authentic cadences in the tonic, and by a bold modulation to D-flat in the second half of the song.

The source for this edition of Rubinstein's *Clärchens Lied* ("Freudvoll und liedvoll") is the first edition (1864): An Frau | Rose v. Milde. | Sechs Lieder | für | eine Singstimme | mit Begleitung des Pianoforte | von | Ant. Rubinstein | op. 57 . . . Leipzig, Verlag von Bartholf Senff. No. 4, plate number 318. 322. Copy in Harvard University Library, Cambridge, MA.

[14] Hans von Bülow (1830–94) began his musical education at the age of nine by studying piano with Clara Schumann's father, the infamous Friedrich Wieck; later he studied counterpoint with Hauptmann in Dresden. As a student of law in Berlin in 1850, Bülow began to write for a local paper and acquired a reputation as a champion of the new school of Liszt and Wagner. As a result of his enthusiasm over the premiere of *Lohengrin*, he abandoned the study of law in favor of music and for the next three years renewed his studies of piano with Liszt in Weimar.

The first of Bülow's many concert tours was made through Germany and Austria in 1853. Two years later he secured a position as pianist at the conservatory in Berlin, where he remained for the next nine years. During these years he wrote a number of articles on musical and political subjects and continued to tour as a pianist and conductor, generally winning acclaim. Called by King Ludwig II, Bülow went to Munich in 1864 and eventually became court kapellmeister. After 1872 he again toured frequently and held musical directorships in Hanover and Meiningen before settling in Hamburg.

During the second half of the century, Bülow was known primarily as a virtuoso pianist and votary of the new German school (he conducted the premiere of Wagner's *Tristan und Isolde*) as well as of Beethoven and Brahms. Under his direction, in 1880–85 the orchestra in Meiningen became one of the most precise in Germany. Between 1852 and 1880 Bülow published thirty works with opus numbers and a small number without, most of which are for piano solo. There are only six volumes of lieder, but these include the first of his published compositions, *Sechs Gedichte*, op. 1, and his last, *Drei Lieder*, op. 30.

Bülow's *Freisinn* is not at all as progressive in its harmonic style as some of his other works, especially those in instrumental genres. The equestrian suggestion of the rhythm of the introduction and afterward is obvious and somewhat commonplace. However, certain other rhythmic figures are rather challenging, especially the cross rhythms between the voice and accompaniment (e.g., mm. 63–64) and among parts of the accompaniment (m. 65).

The source for this edition of Bülow's *Freisinn* ("Laßt mich nur auf meinem Sattel gelten!") is the first edition (1852): Fünf Lieder | für eine hohe Bassstimme | mit Klavierbegleitung | componirt | von | Hans von Bülow | Op. 5. | . . . Hamburg | Fritz Schuberth. No. 1, plate number R. 2643. Copy in Bayerische Staatsbibliothek, Munich, Germany.

[15] At the age of five, the precocious Joseph Rheinberger (1839–1901) began music instruction with an organist in Vaduz. After only two years, during which time he had begun to compose, he took over a position as organist at a local church, and by the age of nine he was performing frequently in public as a pianist. In 1851 Rheinberger moved to Munich to study for two years at the conservatory and remained in that city for the rest of his life. Finding employment as an organist and teacher, he rapidly acquired a reputation as a virtuoso, and in 1859 he began to teach piano and theory at the conservatory. In the same year his op. 1, a collection of keyboard works, was published. As conductor of the Munich Choral Society, 1864–77, Rheinberger exerted influence on the cultivation of sacred music, especially by baroque masters.

During his day, Rheinberger was known above all as an insightful and inspiring teacher, whose pupils included Humperdinck, Wolf-Ferrari, and Furtwängler. His study of music by baroque and classical masters strongly influenced his pedagogy and his own style as a composer. Although in his position as coach at the Munich court opera he was acquainted with Wagner and von Bülow, he was unsympathetic to the new German school. His large list of compositions includes approximately 100 lieder, although he was most successful in his works for organ, for which he wrote twenty sonatas, and in his masses. In their expressive lyricism and restraint, Rheinberger's songs are considerably more intimate and conservative than are most of his other works, especially those for solo organ, which are generally more harmonically adventurous and technically challenging.

Performers of this song may be troubled by the conflicting rhythmic figure of the triplet played against a dotted-eighth and sixteenth, as in measure 8. In the music written earlier in the nineteenth century it may be argued that it is often acceptable to perform such a figure as if the dotted-eighth and sixteenth were a quarter and eighth triplet. However, by the middle of the century, and in this work specifically, it is suggested that the figure be performed exactly as it is written.

The source for this edition of Rheinberger's *Nachtgesang* ("O! gib vom weichen Pfühle") is the first edition (1861): 7 | Lieder | für eine Singstimme | mit Begleitung des Pianoforte | componirt und | Frau Fanny von Hoffnaass | gewidmet von | Josef Rheinberger | op. 3 | 2te Folge der Lieder-Sammlung mit Piano-Forte-Begleitung No. 949 à 955 . . . Mainz bei B. Schott's Söhnen. No. 7. The seven songs were composed between 1857 and

1861; *Nachtgesang* was written on 10 November 1857.[36] Plate number 17192.7. Copy in Bayerische Staatsbibliothek, Munich, Germany.

[16] After briefly studying jurisprudence, Arnold Mendelssohn (1855–1933), the son of a second cousin of Felix Mendelssohn, received his formal education in music at the Institute for Church Music in Berlin from 1877–80. As a composition pupil of Taubert, Mendelssohn quickly developed his own style and published his op. 1, a song on a text by Hans Storm, in 1885. After 1880 he spent two years as music director and organist at the university in Bonn, where he became friends with the music historian Philipp Spitta. Following an appointment as music director in Bielefeld, 1882–85, Mendelssohn spent five years in Cologne as instructor of composition at the conservatory. Finally, in 1891, he accepted a position as professor of church music at the conservatory in Darmstadt, which he held for the rest of his life. After 1912 he also taught at the Frankfurt conservatory, where Hindemith was to become one of his students.

A devoted teacher, Mendelssohn was also known as a gifted pianist and accompanist, especially of his own lieder. His efforts as editor and writer on behalf of baroque music were influential. Among his more than 219 completed compositions are many sacred and secular choral works, orchestral works (including three symphonies), instrumental sonatas, three string quartets, operas, and incidental music for two of Goethe's plays (*Paria* and *Pandora*). Mendelssohn's 170 lieder, many of which became popular during his life, were set to poems by a number of poets, including Heine, Uhland, and Eichendorff, but the largest number of his song texts (at least 55) were drawn from Goethe.[37]

Mendelssohn's songs range in style from the simple and diatonic to the highly complex and chromatic. The two songs of this anthology, *Am Flusse* and *Wer sich der Einsamkeit ergibt*, are in their length and breadth of expression entirely characteristic of his approach to the genre. The consistent, repetitive figures, abrupt and colorful shifts of harmony, and Mendelssohn's broad, arching perspective of tonality, in which the tonic is established at the beginning of the song but not heard again until the end, are typical features of his style. Although *Am Flusse* calls for "Laute" (lute) and may be performed on that instrument, the term may also be taken to mean the generic class of instruments that includes the guitar.

The source for this edition of *Wer sich der Einsamkeit ergibt* is the first edition (1898?): Zweite Folge | der | Lieder und Gesänge | für eine Singstimme | mit | Begleitung des Pianoforte. | von | Arnold Mendelssohn. | . . . Berlin. Verlag von Ries & Erler. No. 3, plate number R. 6973(c) E. Copy in Newberry Library, Chicago, IL.

[17] The source for this edition of *Am Flusse* ("Verfliesset, vielgeliebte Lieder") is the first edition (1904?): Dritte Folge | der | Lieder und Gesänge | für eine Singstimme | mit | Begleitung des Pianoforte. | componirt | von | Arnold Mendelssohn. | . . . Berlin Verlag von Ries & Erler. Plate number R. 7839 E. Copy in Newberry Library, Chicago, IL.

[18] Ferruccio Busoni (1866–1924) was raised near Florence, Italy, in a musical family and received his early instruction from his parents. A child of unusual talent, he gave his first public concert as a pianist at the age of seven, and by ten he had begun to tour, occasionally performing his own compositions. His first published works were two settings of *Ave Maria*, opp. 1 and 2, from 1877. In 1881 he became a member of the Reale Accademia Filarmonica of Bologna. Broader success was achieved in Vienna, where he became friends with Karl Goldmark and Brahms. Upon the recommendation of the latter, Busoni moved to Leipzig in 1886 to study with Carl Reinecke. There, he met Tchaikovsky, Grieg, and Mahler. After brief residences in Helsinki and Moscow and a concert tour in America, Busoni moved to Berlin in 1894 and remained there for the rest of his life.

Busoni published a large number of compositions (many for piano) but only twenty-one songs. These were set to verses by various poets, including Byron, Boito, Uhland, and Goethe. The predominantly chromatic style so typical of his keyboard works is less evident in the humorously allegorical song *Lied des Mephistopheles* ("Es war einmal ein König"), in which the chromaticism is either largely melodic or derives from abrupt juxtapositions of tonal centers.

The source for this edition of *Lied des Mephistopheles* ("Es war einmal ein König") is the first edition (1919): Zwei Gedichte | von Goethe | für eine Baritonstimme und Klavier | von | Ferruccio Busoni. Breitkopf und Härtel. Plate number D.L.V. 3528. Copy in the Hoskins Library, University of Tennessee, Knoxville, TN.

[19] Born in Moscow, Hans Pfitzner (1869–1949) received early training in theory and piano at the conservatory in Frankfurt. Before concluding his studies in 1890, he composed a number of works in various genres, including over forty lieder, some of which were published as opp. 2–7. He found brief appointments at the Koblenz Conservatory, the Mainz Stadttheater, and later the Stern Conservatory in Berlin, from which he resigned in 1899 to reside in Munich. Between 1906 and 1917 Pfitzner was director of the conservatory and conductor of the orchestra in Strassburg. He gained broad recognition upon the successful premiere of his opera *Palestrina* in 1917. He returned to Berlin in 1920 to teach composition at the Prussian Academy. During the early Nazi years he was honored officially, and his works were performed. Toward the end of World War II, however, he became alienated, he was forced to move several times in order to seek safety, and by the war's end he was destitute.

As an accompanist, composer, and musical essayist, Pfitzner was, before his fall from political grace, among the most popular musicians of his day. His list of works includes five operas, twelve orchestral works, concerti, and compositions for choral and chamber ensembles. He was particularly devoted to romantic music, especially to the music of Schumann and Wagner, and to romantic poetry. Of his 106 songs, nineteen are set to texts by Eichendorff (his favorite poet) but only four to poems by Goethe. Pfitzner's op. 26, no. 5, written in Strassburg on 22 August 1916, is representative of the composer's post-romantic style of broad, expressive, diatonic lyricism. Where the poetry demands it, however, Pfitzner's style is chromatic and his lyricism attenuated, as in his setting of "In Danzig".[38]

The source for this edition of *Mailied* ("Wie herrlich leuchtet mir die Natur!") is the first edition (1916): Fünf | Lieder | von | Hans Pfitzner | op. 26 . . . Leipzig: M. Brockhaus. No. 5, plate number M. B. 636ª. Copy in British Museum, London, England.

[20] Justus Hermann Wetzel (1879–1973) studied natural sciences, philosophy, and art history. After training in piano and composition in Berlin, he earned a Ph.D. degree in music at the university in Marburg in 1901. He acquired a reputation as a competent teacher at the Riemann Conservatory in Stettin, 1905–7. From 1926 to 1938 he taught at the Staatliche Akademie für Kirchen- und Schulmusik in Berlin, a position from which he was forced to resign during the war, but to which he was reinstated in 1945. After 1948 he lived in Überlingen as a composer.

As an essayist Wetzel wrote prolifically on a variety of musical subjects and published a text book on music theory (1911). His compositions, which achieved modest popularity during his life, included works for chorus, chamber ensembles, keyboard pieces, and songs (the latter being his most successful). He wrote over 525 lieder, including ones based on melodies from the twelfth to the nineteenth centuries. Many of his works were lost during World War II; others remain unpublished. Most significant are his settings of Hesse, Eichendorff, and 106 songs on the poetry of Goethe. The setting of *An den Mond* demonstrates Wetzel's predilection for chromatic counterpoint and rhythmic flexibility in text setting.

The source for this edition of *An den Mond* ("Füllest wieder Busch und Tal") is the first edition (1932): Justus | Hermann Wetzel | Vierter Liederkreis | für eine Singstimme und Klavier | Gedichte von Goethe | Erstes Heft - Opus 14 | . . . Verlag Albert Stahl - Berlin W 57. No. 10, plate number A. 1134 S. Copy in Yale University Library, New Haven, CT.

[21] A child of a musical family, Nikolay Karlovich Medtner (1880–1951) received his formal musical education in piano at the Moscow Conservatory, 1892–1900, where he studied theory with Anton Arensky. Having promise as a piano virtuoso, he undertook his first European tour upon leaving the conservatory. Although largely self taught, he quickly gained recognition as a composer, publishing his first works in 1894. He continued to perform as a pianist and held a position as instructor of piano at the Moscow Conservatory in 1909 and again 1914–21. He left the Soviet Union in 1921 to tour Europe and, except for a concert tour in 1927, remained in exile for the rest of his life. He lived in Berlin until 1924, then in Paris, where, although befriended by Rachmaninoff, Medtner wrote unsympathetically about the music of his compatriot contemporaries, including Stravinsky. After 1935 he lived in London and continued to perform until 1944, when he grew ill.

In addition to three concertos for piano, Medtner wrote a large number of solo keyboard works, including sonatas and programmatic character pieces. He published 106 songs, many on the poetry of Pushkin and Goethe. Most of his twenty-nine settings of Goethe's poems were gathered into the song cycles of opp. 6, 15, and 18 (1904–9). Medtner's expressively chromatic *Geweihter Platz* confirms his adherence to a late-romantic style, even at a time when the style had been abandoned by many.

This edition of *Geweihter Platz* ("Wenn zu den Reihen der Nymphen") is based on the first edition (1927): N. Medtner | [on left]Sieben | Lieder | nach Dichtungen von | Goethe, Eichendorff und Chamisso | für | Gesang und Pianoforte | Op 46 | [on right] Seven | Songs | Poems by | Goethe, Eichendorff and Chamisso | with | piano accompaniment | Op. 46 | [both followed by listing of contents] . . . Jul. Heinr. Zimmermann | Berlin Leipzig Riga. No. 2. Text in English included. Plate number Z. 11194. Copy in Newberry Library, Chicago, IL.[39] Reprinted by permission of Musikverlag Zimmermann, Frankfurt/Main, Germany.

[22] Receiving his early musical education at the conservatory in Zurich, Othmar Schoeck (1886–1957) showed a precocious aptitude in composition. Before leaving the conservatory in 1907, he had already written many songs, operas, and symphonic works. He became close friends with the poet Hermann Hesse. Following brief studies with Max Reger in Leipzig, Schoeck returned to Zurich in 1908, where he remained the rest of his life. He gained fame as a composer, especially of lieder, and was also very active as an accompanist and conductor of local choral and orchestral ensembles. A few of his larger works were also successful, including the singspiel on Goethe's *Erwin und Elmire*, performed in Zurich in 1916. Because of illness he retired in 1944.

Although Schoeck composed ten works for stage and many choral and orchestral compositions, most of his compositions are songs, of which he wrote nearly 400. His models in this genre were Schubert and Schumann, and he drew often on the poetry of such German romantics as Goethe, Eichendorff, and Uhland.

Schoeck wrote twenty-three songs on poems by Goethe. Those of op. 19a were composed between 1909 and 1914; *Rastlose Liebe* was written in Zurich in 1912 and was first performed on 23 March 1915, in Bern.[40] Schoeck's setting of *Rastlose Liebe* reflects in its disjunct melodic motion, rhythmic intensity, and chromaticism the energy suggested by the poem. Others of Schoeck's songs are more consistently diatonic.[41]

This edition of *Rastlose Liebe* ("Dem Schnee, dem Regen") is based on the following edition: Lieder nach Gedichten von Goethe, für eine Singstimme und Klavier, op. 19a, Breitkopf und Härtel, Leipzig [1926]. No. 5, Dem Schnee, dem Regen (Rastlose Liebe).

Text in French and English included. Plate number 29111. Reprinted by permission of Breitkopf & Härtel, Wiesbaden.

Editorial Method

The sources for the lieder in this anthology are the first published editions or other early prints drawn from several European and American libraries. While some sources have been consulted directly, others have been examined by means of photoduplication.

Although nineteenth-century editions of this repertoire can often be adopted in modern performances without alterations, many sources of that period contain editorial features that are now out of favor, inconsistent, or even misleading. In the present edition, older practices of engraving have been modernized in such matters as barlines, stem directions, the notation of chords, the notation of triplets, the notation of rests, accidentals, and the placement within the score of slurs, dynamics, articulation marks, literal directives, and tempo indications. In addition, the spelling and punctuation of literal directives, tempo indications, etc. have been tacitly modernized and standardized. These changes, insofar as they are unequivocal, are not distinguished in the score. In general, however, the present edition reproduces the readings of the sources as closely as possible, except where the original is unclear or is obviously in error.

Editorial emendations, including the correction of indisputable errors within the sources, are cited in the remarks for the individual songs or are distinguished in the score by means of square brackets. No alterations have been made in such matters as key signatures, meters, beaming, note values, grace notes or ornaments, keyboard fingerings, expression marks, or clefs. In a few cases in which accidentals appear to be lacking in the sources, they have been supplied in square brackets. Cautionary accidentals in the sources have been retained. Only in a few sources (Tomaschek's *Nähe des Geliebten* [3] and his *Das Veilchen* [4], and Medtner's *Geweihter Platz* [21]) are metronome marks indicated, and these have been retained here. The vocal range for each song is indicated at the head of the score. In a few cases in which the sources are inconsistent in sluring or phrasing marks within identical or analogous passages, added slurs are given as dashed slurs ( ). However, where variants in these articulations between parallel phrases affect the character of the phrases, they have not been altered (as in [9], mm. 24–28, 50–54, 74–78).

Published editions of solo songs from the first half of the nineteenth century are not always consistent in providing tempo indications, dynamics, and phrase markings for both the keyboard and the voice. Most early editions provide only a single tempo indication at the head of the score above the voice clef, and dynamics are often omitted from the voice part altogether. In the early editions of Zelter's songs, for example, neither dynamic nor tempo indications are provided. Performers of songs from this anthology may choose to observe more dynamics than those that appear in the source (e.g., to emphasize the melodic contour or to highlight particularly expressive passages of the text). By the second half of the century, composers more often provided their voice parts with individual dynamics, and by the end of the century, voice parts were occasionally given different dynamic indications from those of the accompanying parts, as composers became more exacting in their notation of the balance between voice and keyboard (see [20]).

Older practices of German grammar, particularly those from the first half of the nineteenth century involving orthography and hyphenation, have been altered in this edition to conform to modern usage. Differences in spelling between the poetic source and the text of the song that do not affect the meaning of the text have been modernized but have not been cited in the commentary (e.g., "sein" for "seyn" or "Mut" for "Muth"). In this edition, the capitalization of texts in the song settings has been altered to conform to the poetic models, and these changes have been made without further comment. Throughout this volume, however, the original text underlay in the sources remains otherwise unaltered, even in punctuation, except in cases of obvious error, which are cited in the commentary. The uncommon performance and tempo indications given in German in the sources have been translated in the commentary either into English or into familiar Italian items. Special instructions in the sources are given in both the original German and in English translation on the music page.

While the majority of the poems given here can be recited in their original form by either men or women, a significant number of Goethe's poems were phrased expressly for a woman's voice (e.g., "Nur wer die Sehnsucht kennt" [1]). Especially during the early years of the nineteenth century, composers occasionally altered poems slightly so that they might appropriately be sung by a voice other than that implied by the poem itself.

While a few of the poems set in this anthology were first published in collections of verses ([5], [20], [21], and [22]), some first appeared in novels or plays. It is not uncommon in novels of this period for characters occasionally to sing or recite in verse. Throughout the extensive prose of *Wilhelm Meister*, for example, some of the characters recite or sing lieder (i.e., poems). The most famous of these are the songs of Mignon and the harpist, including "Nur wer die Sehnsucht kennt," "Kennst du das Land?" and "Wer sich der Einsamkeit ergibt" (included here as numbers [1], [6], and [16]). *Faust*, a drama unusually rich in musical references, contains several verses to be sung by Gretchen, Mephistopheles, and other characters of the play, two of which are included here ([9] and [18]). The poem "Freudvoll und leidvoll" ([13]) originally appeared within the text of the drama *Egmont*; the famous *Erlkönig* ([8]) appeared first within the text of a singspiel; *Nähe des Geliebten* ([3] and [11]) was written for the drama *Claudine von Villa Bella*. Three of the poems of this anthology ([2], [10], and [17]) were first published in Schiller's journal *Musen-Almanach*.

An unrhymed, line-by-line literal translation is given for each poem in Texts and Translations. The reader may also wish to consult translations provided in other references, for example in *The Fischer-Dieskau Book of Lieder*, translated by George Bird and Richard Stokes (New York, 1977). It may occasionally be beneficial for the performer to consult other word-for-word translations, as in Berton Coffin, Werner Singer, and Pierre Delathe, *Word-by-Word Translations of Songs and Arias* (New York, 1966), or Lois Phillips, *Lieder Line by Line* (London, 1979). Although the major novels and plays have often been translated, a uniform English translation of Goethe's complete works is still unavailable.[42]

As Goethe's poetry became so extraordinarily popular within musical circles throughout the nineteenth century, it is not surprising that the poems represented in this anthology were also set by many others. Comparisons among these various settings can be instructive and may provide insight into both the poem itself as well as the composers' styles and interpretations. Lists of other settings of these poems can be found in Willi Schuh's *Goethe-Vertonungen: Ein Verzeichnis* (Zürich, 1952); additional early nineteenth-century settings are cited in Ernst Challiers's *Grosser Lieder-Katalog* (Berlin, 1885).

Critical Notes

The critical notes give a description of the variants between the musical sources and the present edition. The following abbreviations have been used: m(m) = measure(s); kb. = keyboard; v. = voice; vl. = violin; r.h. = right hand; l.h. = left hand. Pitches are referred to according to the system in which c' = middle C, c" = the C above middle C, c = the C below middle C, etc.

[1] *Sehnsucht (Carl Zelter)*

M. 1, 4, kb., accent on first beat provided only for upper staff.

COMMENTS For the anacrusis it is likely that Zelter intended the lower part of the r.h. to slur with the upper part, as the beaming in m. 1 suggests. The pianist may wish to alter the slurs of mm. 4–5 and of parallel passages, slurring to the first beat of the measure, as in mm. 1–2, and may choose to add slurs in mm. 9–11, 18–19. The editor suggests a return to *Tempo primo* at m. 20, note 2.

[2] *Das Blümlein Wunderschön (Johann Rudolf Zumsteeg)*

M. 9, kb., l.h., d-sharp printed as quarter note. M. 10, kb., in source accent on first beat appears between staves.

COMMENTS M. 15, kb., *mf* implies accents. Mm. 29, 30, editor recommends that v. observe dynamic indications in kb.

[3] *Nähe des Geliebten (Wenzel Johann Tomaschek)*

Metronome mark is given as "Mälzl. 60. ♩". (Johann Nepomuk Maelzel was the inventor of the pendulum metronome. He manufactured and sold them in Paris under the name of Mälzl & Cie.) M. 2, kb., r.h., e-flat lacks dot. M. 58, kb., r.h., slur extends only to 5th note (see l.h.).

[4] *Das Veilchen (Wenzel Johann Tomaschek)*

Metronome mark is given as "Mälzel. 66 ♩". (See notes for [3].) M. 40, kb., r.h., natural sign in front of e' rather than g'. M. 55, metronome mark is given as "Mälzel 160 ♩". (See notes for [3].)

COMMENTS Singer may wish to follow the dynamic indications of the accompaniment throughout. The editor suggests that the figures in mm. 11, 17, 25, and 51 all be interpreted as four even sixteenth notes. The third beat of m. 54 might also be performed in this manner. Likewise the first beat of m. 62 should be performed as two even eighth notes.

[5] *Die Spinnerin (Ferdinand Ries)*

M. 34, kb., *cresc.* in source relocated to m. 33, as in m. 18.

[6] *Mignons Lied (Louis Spohr)*

It is difficult to distinguish in the source between accents in the kb. and short descrendo marks. These have been interpreted as descrendo marks to correspond to v. M. 17, ¾ lacking in source. M. 30, kb., l.h., precautionary natural in front of a.

[7] *Der Fischer (Moritz Hauptmann)*

The complete absence of dynamic markings in v. throughout poses special problems for the performer. Dynamics in vl. and kb. in source retained, even where these do not agree (as in m. 5). M. 15, vl., source gives *ten.* over both double-stops; removed here to conform with kb. and with m. 23. The singer may wish to observe dynamics more consistently with those given in the kb., including *cresc.* and *dimin.*

[8] *Der Erlkönig (Bernhard Klein)*

Mm. 31–32, 59–60, kb. has double stems. M. 39, kb., r.h., stem joins f" to f', f-sharp" to f-sharp'. M. 51, kb., l.h., lacks treble clef. Mm. 58, 82, 107, v., tempo indication printed in the following measure. M. 75, kb., l.h., c is dotted. M. 107, v., *p* given at beginning of next measure. M. 114, v., last note is quarter instead of eighth.

COMMENTS Mm. 34–50, 66–82, 98–107, kb., 𝄢 . . . * does not necessarily indicate that the passage should be played all with one pedal, but that the pedal should be used with discretion (especially on a modern instrument).

[9] *Der König von Thule (Heinrich Marschner)*

The inconsistency of slurring between mm. 17 and 63, kb., has been accepted because of differences in syllabification of text. Inconsistencies of articulation in the source between (kb.) mm. 24ff., 50ff., 74ff. have been retained.

[10] *Der Zauberlehrling (Carl Loewe)*

M. 8, v., source has c"–d-flat" trill on beat four, as in kb., r.h. (altered to parallel m. 23). M. 8, kb., beat 2, l.h., g–b printed without beam, as in v. M. 34, kb., r.h., note 11, and v., note 6, source has sharp. Mm. 39–40, kb., slur over both measures broken to parallel mm. 9–10, 24–25. M. 42, kb., l.h., beat 3, chord is c′–f′. M. 83, kb., l.h., natural sign placed on c′ instead of e′.

[11] *Nähe des Geliebten (Ferdinand Hiller)*

COMMENTS Performers may wish to observe *mf* in m. 32 (parallel to mm. 2, 17), and *p* in m. 57.

[12] *Wonne der Wehmut (Robert Franz)*

No notes.

[13] *Clärchens Lied (Anton Rubinstein)*

M. 17, v., b♭′ dotted eighth lacks syllable -*le*.

[14] *Freisinn (Hans von Bülow)*

No notes.

[15] *Nachtgesang (Joseph Rheinberger)*

COMMENTS The editor recommends that where a triplet is to be played against a dotted-eighth, sixteenth rhythm, the latter be performed so that the sixteenth corresponds to the last note of the triplet (see mm. 8, 15, 19–21).

[16] *Wer sich der Einsamkeit ergibt (Arnold Mendelssohn)*

M. 20, kb., r.h., 5th chord, a-flat′ and b-natural′ (see m. 46). M. 47, kb., r.h., 5th chord, a′-flat rather than g′-flat (see m. 21).

[17] *Am Flusse (Arnold Mendelssohn)*

At head of score: "Frau LILLI BEHRENS freundschaftlich gewidmet von O . . . . A . . . . ."

[18] *Lied des Mephistopheles (Ferruccio Busoni)*

Head of score indicates "An Dr. Augustus Milner."

[19] *Mailied (Hans Pfitzner)*

M. 42, v., kb., *rit.* on second half of second beat in both parts. Performers may interpret the phrase "Wieder leicht bewegt" (m. 48) to mean "tempo primo."

[20] *An den Mond (Justus Hermann Wetzel)*

No notes.

[21] *Geweihter Platz (Nikolay Karlovich Medtner)*

M. 24, kb., beat 3, pedal release sign (*) appears under note 16.

[22] *Rastlose Liebe (Othmar Schoeck)*

English and French translations of tempo indications and of text appear in source. V. may wish to follow kb. dynamics more closely throughout.

Acknowledgments

Support from the Research Grants Committee of Northwestern University during preliminary research for this edition is gratefully acknowledged. The musical sources for this edition have been drawn from several European and American libraries. The cooperation of the following libraries is sincerely appreciated: Bayerische Staatsbibliothek (Munich, Germany); Boston Public Library (Boston, MA); British Museum (London, England); Library of Congress, Music Division (Washington, D.C.); University of California, Berkeley, Music Library (Berkeley, CA); Gesellschaft der Musikfreunde (Vienna, Austria); Harvard University Library (Cambridge, MA); Hoskins Library, University of Tennessee (Knoxville, TN); New York Public Library (New York, NY); Newberry Library (Chicago, IL); Staatsbibliothek, Preußischer Kulturbesitz (Berlin, Germany); Yale University Library (New Haven, CT).

Notes

1. See Hans Pyritz, *Goethe-Bibliographie,* ed. Heinz Nicolai and Gerhard Burkhardt, 2 vols. (Heidelberg: Carl Winter, Universitätsverlag, 1965–68). The bibliography contains an extensive section on music.

2. For example, in his edition *Gedichte von Goethe in Kompositionen seiner Zeitgenossen,* Shriften der Goethe-Gesellschaft, vol. 11 (Weimar: Goethe-Gesellschaft 1896), Max Friedlaender includes four different settings of *Heidenröslein* and six of *Erlkönig.*

3. "Von Allem, was später gesungen worden ist, kann nur das auf den Namen eines wahrhaften Liedes Anspruch machen, was, als freie Naturstimme, in wohllautender Sprache und sangbarer Form ein schönes Gefühl zur Anschauung bringt. Anmuthige, gefällig geschwätzige Oberflächlichkeit, die man seit Hagedorn, nach Frankreichs Vorgange, under den Deutschen eine Zeit lang als Wesen des Liedes dahinnahm, konnte den deutschen Sinne nicht lange zusagen. Das wahre Lied verschmäht auch die Tiefe nicht. Solche Lieder gab zuerst Göthe den Deutschen wieder, und es möchte nicht zu viel gesagt sein, wenn wir behaupten, daß seit dieser Zeit von Deutschland aus die Erkenntniß des Wesens aller Liederpoesie sich über die übrigen Literaturländer Europas verbreitet habe"; *Allgemeine deutsche Real-Encyklopädie für die gebildeten Stände (Conversations-Lexikon),* 8th ed. (Leipzig: Brockhaus, 1835), 6:642–43. Unless otherwise stated, all translations are mine.

4. "Es ist für den Tonsetzer eine Hauptregel, sowol in der Vokal- als Instrumentalmusik kantabel, das ist, singend zu setzen. . . . Will der Tonsetzer hierin glüklich seyn, so muß er vor allen Dingen selbst singen können"; Johann Georg Sulzer, *Allgemeine Theorie der schönen Künste,* 3d ed. (Frankfurt, 1798), 4:424. It is commonly held that Sulzer, being untutored in music, relied on either Johann Kirnberger or J. A. P. Schulz for articles on this subject.

5. See Goethe's letter to Auguste Gräfin, 21 September 1775, in which Sulzer is referred to as a man "von Geist." Goethe was influenced by Sulzer's lexicon most obviously in the writing of his essay "Von deutscher Baukunst" (1823); see Goethe, *Gedenkausgabe der Werke, Briefe und Gespräche,* ed. Ernst Beutler, vol. 21, *Brief der Jahre 1814–1832* (Zurich: Artemis, 1949), 292, 1035, 1264 (hereafter referred to as *Gedenkausgabe*).

6. "Denn hier kommt es nicht auf die Belustigung des Ohres an, nicht auf die Bewundrung [sic] der Kunst, nicht auf die Ueberraschung durch künstliche Harmonien und schwere Modulationen; sondern lediglich auf Rührung"; Sulzer, 3:301.

7. "Mit diesem Namen bezeichnet man überhaupt jedes lyrische Gedicht von mehrern Strophen, welches zum Gesange bestimmt, und mit einer solchen Melodie verbunden ist, die bey jeder Strophe wiederholt wird, und die zugleich die Eigenschaft hat, daß sie von jedem Menschen, der gesunde und nicht ganz unbiegsame Gesangorgane besitzt, ohne Rücksicht auf künstliche Ausbildung derselben, vorgetragen werden kann. Hieraus folgt, daß die Melodie eines Liedes weder einem so weiten Umfang der Töne, noch solche Singmanieren und Sylbendehnung enthalten darf, wodurch sich bloß der künstliche und ausgebildete Gesang der Arie auszeichnet, sondern daß der Ausdruck der in dem Texte enthaltenen Empfindung durch einfache, aber desto treffendere Mittel erlangt werden muß"; Heinrich Christoph Koch, *Musikalisches Lexikon* (1802; reprint, Hildesheim: Georg Olms, 1964), 901f.

8. "Die Melodie der Ballade, deren Charaker von dem Inhalte des Gedichtes bestimmt wird, ist weder an eine besondere Form, noch an eine besondere Taktart gebunden. Seit einiger Zeit hat man angefangen, sie nicht so, wie bey dem Liede, mit jeder Strophe des Textes zu wiederholen, sondern den Text ganz durch zu komponiren"; Koch, 212–13.

9. "Das Lied . . . ist der reinste Ausfluß unserer Gefühle in der einfachsten Form gegeben; es redet die Sprache der Wahrheit in einem reizenden Gewande und findet sein Echo in unserem Herzen. . . . Der Componist muß im Liede die üppigsten Blüthen seiner Phantasie niederlegen; . . . der Sänger muß seine innersten Gefühle, die Geheimnisse seines Herzens in den Tönen ausströmen lassen. Das Lied ist der Hausfreund deutscher Häuslichkeit; der Triumph der Musik im Kreise befreundeter Geister. . . . Die kritischen Anforderungen an das musikalische Lied sind Schönheit und Sangbarkeit der Melodie, natürliche, aber interessante Harmoniefolge, charakteristische und den Gesang hebende Begleitung. Hinsichtlich der Form der Lieder hat man die Freiheit der Poesie endlich auch in der Musik aufgenommen; dennoch wird die einfachste Urform, wie wir sie in Volksliedern finden, zu allen Zeiten ihre Herrschaft behaupten"; C. Herleßsohn, ed., *Dammenkonversationslexikon* (Leipzig: Herleßsohn und Lühe, 1836), 6:361–62. The article was signed by "-k." and may have been written by Schumann's acquaintance, Karl Banck, who reviewed vocal music for Schumann's journal, *Die Neue Zeitschrift für Musik,* and was himself a composer of songs.

10. Carl Dahlhaus, for example, considers the year of Schubert's "Gretchen am Spinnrade" (1814) a significant turning point in the history of the lied, as it began then to include a greater variety of formal types than was common in the strophic forms of the previous generation; see *Die Musik des 19. Jahrhunderts,* Neues Handbuch der Musikwissenschaft, vol. 6 (Wiesbaden: Athenaion, 1980), 81.

11. "Hr. Fr. S. schreibt keine eigentlichen Lieder und will keine schreiben . . . , sondern freye Gesänge, manchmal so frey, daß man sie allenfalls Capricen oder Phantasien nennen kann"; "Recension," *Allgemeine Musikalische Zeitung* 26 (1824): 426, cited in Dahlhaus, *Die Musik des 19. Jahrhunderts,* 80.

12. All three designations can be found among the works of both Schumann and Brahms. See, for example, Schumann's *Fünf Lieder* (Anderson, Chamisso), op. 37, *Drei Gesänge* (Chamisso), op. 31, and *Drei Gedichte* (Geibel), op. 30.

13. Robert Schumann, "Neue Symphonieen für Orchester," *Neue Zeitschrift für Musik* 11 (1839): 2; Hugo Wolf, in *The Music Criticism of Hugo Wolf,* tr. H. Pleasants (New York: Homes and Meier, 1978), 273 (originally appeared in *Wiener Salonblatt,* 3 April 1887).

14. *Hugo Riemanns Musik-Lexikon,* edited by Alfred Einstein, 9th ed. (Berlin: Max Hesses Verlag, 1919), 677.

15. From 1810 until the end of his life, Goethe tried unsuccessfully to write a *Tonlehre,* as a complement to his *Farbenlehre,* in order to explain principles of acoustics and music theory, but never progressed beyond rudimentary observations. See Hans Joachim Moser, "Goethe und die Musikalische Akustik," in *Zum 90. Geburtstage . . . Rochus freiherrn von Liliencron . . .* (Berlin: H. Brücker, 1910).

16. "Die Würde der Kunst erscheint bei der Musik vielleicht am eminentesten, weil sie keinen Stoff hat, der abgerechnet werden müßte. Sie ist ganz Form und Gehalt und erhört und veredelt alles, was sie ausdrückt"; *Goethes Werke,* ed. Erich Trunz (Hamburg: Christian Wegner, 1950), 8:290.

17. See, for example, Goethe's letter to Zelter, 24 August 1823, in *Gedenkausgabe* vol. 21.

18. "Nichts und Alles. Nichts! wie er es durch die äußern Sinne empfängt darf er nachahmen; aber Alles darf er darstellen was er bei diesen äußern Sinneseinwirkungen empfindet. . . . Das Innere in Stimmung zu setzen, ohne die

gemeinen äußern Mittel zu brauchen ist der Musik großes und edles Vorrecht"; letter to Adalbert Schöpke, 16 February 1818, in *Gedenkausgabe*, 21:275. Schopenhauer's *Die Welt als Wille und Vorstellung*, which appeared in the same year as Goethe's remarks, contains similar statements on music's ability to move the soul without the aid of the intellect.

19. "Melodien, Gänge und Läufe ohne Worte und Sinn scheinen mir Schmetterlingen oder schönen bunten Vögeln ähnlich zu sein, die in der Luft vor unsern Augen herumschweben die wir allenfalls haschen und uns zueignen möchten; da sich der Gesang dagegen wie ein Genius gen Himmel hebt und das bessere Ich in uns hin zu begleiten anreizt"; *Goethes Werke*, 7:128. Goethe's thoughts on the inability of instrumental music to express rational thoughts articulately resemble certain of Wagner's statements on the subject made over fifty years later.

20. In a letter to Friedrich Unger, 5 August 1799, he suggested that it would be of great advantage in the publication of a new volume of poems if they could be accompanied by original melodies from Zelter; see *Gedenkausgabe*, 19:380–81.

21. According to the tenor Wilhelm Ehlers (1774–1845), Goethe became convinced during successive performances of a lied that it was possible to perform a melody so as to accommodate the text from strophe to strophe. A similar event was related by the singer Eduard Genast in 1824; see Willi Reich, *Goethe und die Musik: Aus den Werken, Briefen und Gesprächen* (Zurich: Ex Libris, 1949), 56. It may be that many of the songs from the first third of the nineteenth century in modified strophic form may have been conceived in strict strophic form but were written to reflect the contemporary practice of strophic variation.

22. See Leo Balet and E. Gerhard, *Die Verbürlichung der deutschen Kunst, Literatur und Musik im 18. Jahrhundert*, ed. Gert Mattenklott (Frankfurt: Ullstein, 1973), 390ff. The first public performance of a lied by Schubert, for example, was given on 28 February 1819. The song was a setting of Goethe's *Schäfers Klagelied*, D. 121; see Otto Erich Deutsch, *Franz Schubert: Thematisches Verzeichnis seiner Werke in chronologischer Folge* (Kassel: Bärenreiter, 1978), 86.

23. "[D]aß es nicht so sehr auf die Schönheit des Singorgans dabei ankomme, als vielmehr auf die jedesmalige, an gehöriger Stelle angebrachte Betonung, wodurch erst das Lied seine volle Wirkung tut"; letter of 6 August 1822; *Gedenkausgabe*, 23:220.

24. *Johann Wolfgang Goethe Sämtliche Werke*, vol. 14, *Gedichte 1756–1799*, ed. Karl Eibl (Frankfurt: Deutscher Klassiker Verlag, 1987), 1213.

25. "Mir ist zwar von der Natur . . . eine glückliche Stimme versagt, aber innerlich scheint mir oft ein geheimer Genius etwas Rhythmisches vorzuflüstern, so daß ich mich beim Wandern jedesmal im Takt bewege und zugleich leise Töne zu vernehmen glaube, wodurch denn irgend ein Lied begleitet wird, das sich mir auf eine oder die andere Weise gefällig vergegenwärtigt"; *Gedenkausgabe*, 8:336.

26. "Man studiere also unsere herrlichen Volksmelodien, deren Wirkung sich schon über mehr als ein Jahrhundert verbreitet haben; dann erst wird man ein Lied setzen, das unser Volk aufnimmt"; C. F. D. Schubart, *Ideen zu einer Aesthetik der Tonkunst* (Vienna: J. Degen, 1806), 355.

27. J. W. Smeed, *German Song and its Poetry, 1740–1900* (London: Droom Helm, 1987), 165.

28. Max Friedländer, "Die Entstehung der Müllerlieder," *Deutsche Rundschau* 73 (1892–93): 301–7.

29. See Edward Kravitt, "The Orchestral Lied: An Inquiry into its Style and Unexpected Flowering Around 1900," *Music Review* 37 (1976): 209–26.

30. In his early autobiographical sketches (written before 1800), Zelter briefly described what he called an "enduring and trustworthy" friendship with Goethe; see Johann-Wolfgang Schottländer, ed., *Carl Friedrich Zelter: Darstellung seines Lebens*, vol. 44 of *Schriften der Goethe-Gesellschaft* (Weimar: Goethe-Gesellschaft, 1931; reprint, Hildesheim: Georg Olms, 1978), 198.

31. See Ludwig Landshoff, *Johann Rudolph Zumsteeg* (Berlin: S. Fischer, n.d.), 182–87.

32. Hugo Riemann, *Musik Lexikon*, 12th ed., ed. Wilibald Gurlitt (Mainz: B. Schott's Söhne, 1961), 803.

33. The account of Tomaschek's meeting with Goethe is contained in the former's autobiography, a portion of which appears in "Excerpts from the memoirs of J. W. Tomaschek," trans. Abram Loft, *Musical Quarterly* 32 (1946): 244–64.

34. *The New Grove Dictionary of Music and Musicians*, s.v. "Loewe, (Johann) Carl (Gottfried)," by Maurice J. E. Brown.

35. *Die Musik in Geschichte und Gegenwart*, s.v. "Rubinstein, Anton Grigorewitsch," by Guido Walkmann.

36. Hans-Josef Irmen, *Thematisches Verzeichnis der musikalischen Werke Gabriel Josef Rheinbergers* (Regensburg: Gustav Bosse, 1974), 30.

37. See Arnold Werner-Jensen, *Arnold Mendelssohn als Liederkomponist* (Winterthur: Amadeus, 1976), 26–29.

38. See Jurgen Thym, ed., *100 Years of Eichendorff Songs*, Recent Researches in the Music of the Nineteenth and Early Twentieth Centuries, vol. 5 (Madison: A-R Editions, Inc., 1983), 57–60.

39. This song is also published in *Nikolay Karlovich Metner: Sobranie Sochinenii* [collected edition], vol. 6 (Moscow: Gos. Muzykal'noe Izd-vo, 1959–63).

40. Werner Vogel, *Thematisches Verzeichnis der Werke von Othmar Schoeck* (Zurich: Atlantis, 1956), 46–47.

41. Two songs by Schoeck on poetry of Eichendorff are given in Thym, *100 Years of Eichendorff Songs*, 61–67.

42. The translation by Sir Theodore Martin, *Johann Wolfgang von Goethe: Works*, ed. Nathan H. Dole, 14 vols. (Boston: Francis A. Niccolls, 1901–2), includes many of the significant works but takes excessive liberties with the original text.

Texts and Translations

This section is organized as follows: (a) the text of the poem drawn from the music source (see Editorial Method), (b) the editor's translation of the poem, and (c) the citation of the first publication of the poem. For any editorial changes made to the texts (other than those described in Editorial Method), the source readings are given in the COMMENTS section.

Throughout the following discussion the abbreviation *GW* is used to refer to *Goethes Werke*, 133 vols. (Weimar, 1887–1919; reprint, 1975). For descriptions of the variants among poetic sources (e.g., manuscripts, first editions, revised editions), the reader may wish to consult appropriate volumes of *Lesarten* from that edition.

[1] *Sehnsucht (Carl Zelter)*

Nur wer die Sehnsucht kennt,
Weiß, was ich leide!
Allein und abgetrennt
Von aller Freude,
Seh' ich an's Firmament
Nach jener Seite.
Ach, der mich liebt und kennt,
Ist in der Weite.
Es schwindet mir, es brennt
Mein Eingeweide.
Nur wer die Sehnsucht kennt,
Weiß, was ich leide!

Only he who knows longing,
Knows what I suffer!
Alone and removed
From all joy,
(5) I gaze at the firmament
On the other side.
Ah, he who loves and knows me,
Is far away.
I am dizzy,
(10) My body burns.
Only he who knows longing,
Knows what I suffer!

SOURCE OF TEXT: "Nur wer die Sehnsucht kennt," from *Wilhelm Meisters Lehrjahre* (1796), book IV, ch. 11 (an irregular [*unregelmäßiges*] duet with Mignon and the harpist), in *Wilhelm Meisters Theatralische Sendungen*, vol. 6, 1785 (*GW*, 22:67).

[2] *Das Blümlein Wunderschön (Johann Rudolf Zumsteeg)*

[Graf]
Ich kenn' ein Blümlein Wunderschön
Und trage darnach Verlangen,
Ich möcht' es gerne zu suchen gehn,
Allein ich bin gefangen;
Die Schmerzen sind mir nicht gering,
Denn als ich in der Freiheit ging,
Da hatt' ich es in der Nähe.

Von diesem ringsum steilen Schloß
Lass ich die Augen schweifen,
Und kann's vom hohen Thurmgeschoß
Mit Blicken nicht ergreifen,
Und wer mir's vor die Augen brächt,
Es wäre Ritter oder Knecht,
Der sollte mein Trauter bleiben.

Rose
Ich blühe schön und höre dies
Hier unter deinem Gitter,
Du meinest mich, die Rose, gewiß
Du edler armer Ritter.

Count
I know a flower of lovely beauty
And yearn for it dearly;
I'd like to go searching for it,
But I am imprisoned.
(5) My sorrows are not slight,
For when I was at liberty,
I held it close by me.

From this steep encircled castle
I cast my eyes about,
(10) And from the high castle tower
Cannot find it in sight;
And he who brings it before my eyes,
Be he knight or servant,
Will remain my dearest.

Rose
(15) I blossom fair, and hear this
Here under your window.
You mean me, the rose, for sure,
You poor noble knight!

Du hast gar einen hohen Sinn,
Es herrscht die Blumenkönigin
Gewiß auch in deinem Herzen.

Graf

Dein Purpur ist aller Ehren wert,
Im grünen Überkleide,
Darob das Mädchen dein begehrt,
Wie Gold und Edelgeschmeide.
Dein Kranz erhöht das schönste Gesicht,
Allein du bist das Blümchen nicht
Das ich im Stillen verehre.

Lilie

Das Röschen hat gar stolzen Brauch
Und strebet immer nach oben,
Doch wird ein liebes Liebchen auch
Der Lilie Zierde loben.
Wenn's Herze schlägt in treuer Brust,
Und ist sich rein, wie ich, bewußt,
Der hält mich wohl am höchsten.

Graf

Ich nenne mich zwar keusch und rein
Und rein von bösen Fehlen,
Doch muß ich hier gefangen sein
Und muß mich einsam quälen.
Du bist mir zwar ein schönes Bild
Von mancher Jungfrau rein und mild,
Doch weiß ich noch 'was Liebers.

Nelke

Das mag wohl ich die Nelke sein,
Hier in des Wächters Garten,
Wie würde sonst der Alte mein
Mit so viel Sorgen warten?
Im schönen Kreis der Blätter Drang,
Und Wohlgeruch das Leben lang,
Und alle tausend Farben.

Graf

Die Nelke soll man nicht verschmähn,
Sie ist des Gärtners Wonne,
Bald muß sie in dem Lichte stehn,
Bald schützt er sie vor Sonne,
Doch was den Grafen glücklich macht
Es ist nicht ausgesuchte Pracht,
Es ist ein stilles Blümchen.

Veilchen

Ich steh' verborgen und gebückt,
Und mag nicht gerne sprechen,
Doch will ich, weil sich's eben schickt,
Mein tiefes Schweigen brechen,
Wenn ich es bin, du guter Mann,
Wie schmerzt mich's, daß ich hinauf nicht kann,
Dir alle Gerüche senden.

Graf

Das gute Veilchen schätz' ich sehr,
Es ist so gar bescheiden,
Und duftet so schön, doch brauch' ich mehr
In meinen herben Leiden,
Ich will es euch nur eingestehn

(20) You have truly a lofty spirit,
The flower-queen rules
Most certainly in your heart.

Count

Your purple is worthy of all praise
In dress of green;
(25) And so the maid does treasure you,
Like gold and precious jewelry.
Your wreath adorns a most beautiful face:
Alas you are not the little flower,
That I in silence adore.

Lily

The little rose is proud as usual
(30) And tries forever to rise;
But a loving sweetheart will also
Praise the lily's charms.
The heart that beats in a truthful breast
And is consciously pure, like me,
(35) Will value me the most.

Count

I consider myself chaste and pure indeed,
And free from grievous faults;
But here must I remain a prisoner,
And must alone be tormented.
(40) To me you are certainly a pretty picture
Of many a maid, pure and mild:
Yet I know of one more dear.

Carnation

It must be me, the carnation,
Here in the warden's garden;
(45) Why else would he
Wait for me with such worry?
Into a beauteous ring my petals press,
And smell sweet my life long,
And thousands of colors.

Count

(50) One should not slight the carnation;
It is the gardener's delight.
It must now stand in the light;
Now he shades it from the sun;
Yet what makes the count happy
(55) Is not outward splendor:
It is a silent little flower.

Violet

Here I stand hidden and bent,
And would rather not speak.
Yet I shall, since now's the time,
(60) To break my deep silence.
If I am the one, you worthy man,
How it grieves me that I cannot
Send up all aromas to you.

Count

The lovely violet I greatly treasure.
(65) It is so very modest
And smells so fine; yet I need more
In my bitter grief.
I must confess to you:

Auf diesen dürren Felsenhöh'n	Upon these rocky heights
Ist's Liebchen nicht zu finden.	(70) The beloved shall not be found.
Doch wandelt unten an dem Bach	There roams near the stream below
Das treuste Weib der Erde,	The truest woman of the earth,
Und seufzet leise manches Ach,	Who sighs many a gentle ah
Bis ich erlöset werde.	Until I am released.
Wenn sie ein blaues Blümchen bricht	(75) When she breaks a blue floweret
Und immer sagt: Vergiß mein nicht!	And says: Forget me not!
So fühl' ich's in der Ferne.	I feel it from this distance.
Ja in der Ferne fühlt sich die Macht	Even in the distance the force is felt,
Wenn zwei sich redlich lieben,	When two love each other sincerely;
D'rum bin ich in des Kerkers Nacht	(80) In the night of prison I have by this
Auch noch lebendig geblieben,	Remained yet alive.
Und wenn mir fast das Herze bricht,	And when my heart is nearly broken,
So ruf' ich nur: Vergiß mein nicht!	Then I merely cry: forget me not!
Da komm' ich wieder ins Leben.	And I come back to live again.

SOURCE OF TEXT: "Ich kenn' ein Blümlein Wunderschön," from Schiller's *Musen-Almanach für das Jahr 1799* (GW, 1:172–75).

[3] *Nähe des Geliebten* (Wenzel Johann Tomaschek)

Ich denke dein, wenn mir der Sonne Schimmer	I think of you when to me the sun's glimmer
Vom Meere strahlt;	Shines from the sea;
Ich denke dein, wenn sich des Mondes Flimmer	I think of you when the moon's shimmer
In Quellen mahlt.	Is painted in the streams.
Ich sehe dich, wenn auf dem fernen Wege	(5) I see you when on the distant road
Der Staub sich hebt;	The dust rises;
In tiefer Nacht, wenn auf dem schmalen Stege	In the deep of night when on the narrow path
Der Wandrer bebt.	The traveller shivers.
Ich höre dich, wenn dort mit dumpfem Rauschen	I hear you when there with muffled roar
Die Welle steigt.	(10) The wave mounts.
Im stillen Haine geh' ich oft zu lauschen,	In the still woods I often go to listen
Wenn alles schweigt.	When all is silent.
Ich bin bei dir, du seist auch noch so ferne,	I am with you, be you still so far,
Du bist mir nah'!	You are beside me!
Die Sonne sinkt, bald leuchten mir die Sterne.	(15) The sun sets, soon upon me the stars will shine.
O wärst du da!	Oh were you only here!

SOURCE OF TEXT: "Ich denke dein, wenn mir der Sonne Schimmer," from the song album for *Claudine von Villa Bella*, 1795 (GW, 1:58).

COMMENTS: line 9, seventh word is "dumpfen."

[4] *Das Veilchen* (Wenzel Johann Tomaschek)

Ein Veilchen auf der Wiese stand,	A violet stood in the meadow,
Gebückt in sich und unbekannt;	Bent inward and unknown;
Es war ein herzig's Veilchen.	It was a dear violet.
Da kam eine junge Schäferin,	There came a young shepherdess,
Mit leichtem Schritt und munterm Sinn,	(5) With a light step and gay spirit,
Daher, daher,	Through, through,
Die Wiese her, und sang.	Through the meadow, and sang.
Ach! denkt das Veilchen, wär' ich nur	Ah, the violet thinks, if only I were
Die schönste Blume der Natur,	The most beautiful flower of nature,
Ach, nur ein kleines Weilchen,	(10) Ah, for only a brief moment,
Bis mich das Liebchen abgepflückt,	Until my beloved plucked me
Und an dem Busen matt gedrückt!	And pressed me flat to her breast!
Ach nur, ach nur,	Ah only, ah only
Ein Viertelstündchen lang!	For just a quarter hour!

Ach! aber ach! das Mädchen kam,	(15) Ah! but ah! the girl came
Und nicht in acht das Veilchen nahm,	And gave the violet no heed,
Ertrat das arme Veilchen.	Crushed, the poor violet
Es sank und starb und freut' sich noch:	Sank and died and yet was happy.
Und sterb' ich denn, so sterb' ich doch	And though I die, I die yet
Durch sie, durch sie,	(20) Through her, through her,
Zu ihren Füßen doch.	At her feet!

SOURCE OF TEXT: "Ein Veilchen auf der Wiese stand," from *Iris* (1775) (*GW*, 1:164).

[5] Die Spinnerin (Ferdinand Ries)

Als ich still und ruhig spann	As I spun calm and still
Ohne nur zu stocken	Without even pausing,
Trat ein schöner junger Mann	A handsome young man
Nahe mir zum Rocken.	Approached my spinning wheel.
Lobte was zu loben war,	(5) He praised what was to be praised,
Konnte das was schaden?	Could that bring harm?
Mein dem Flachse gleiches Haar,	My flaxen-like hair,
Und den gleichen Faden.	And the similar thread.
Ruhig war er nicht dabei	He was not content in this,
Ließ es nicht beim Alten;	(10) Left it not as it was,
Und der Faden riß entzwei,	And tore the thread in two,
Den ich lang erhalten.	That I had had so long.
Und des Flachses Stein-Gewicht,	And the flax's stone-like weight
Gab noch viele Zahlen;	Was still greatly valued;
Aber ach! ich konnte nicht	(15) But I could no longer
Mehr mit ihnen prahlen.	Boast of it.
Als ich sie zum Weber trug,	When I took it to the weaver,
Fühlt' ich was sich regen,	I felt something stir,
Und mein armes Herze schlug	And my poor heart throbbed
Mit geschwindern Schlägen.	(20) With more rapid beats.
Nun beim heißen Sonnenstich,	Now, with the heat of sunstroke,
Bring' ich's auf die Bleiche	I bring the thread to bleach,
Und mit Mühe bück' ich mich	And with effort I stoop
Nach dem nächsten Teiche.	Toward the next pool.
Was ich in dem Kämmerlein,	(25) What in my little room I
Still und fein gesponnen,	Quietly have spun so fine,
Kommt, wie kann es anders sein?	Comes—how could it be otherwise?—
Endlich an die Sonnen.	At last to light.

SOURCE OF TEXT: "Als ich still und ruhig spann," from *Göthe's neue Schriften*, 7 vols. (Berlin: Unger, 1792–1800), in vol. 7 (1800), p. 63, *Balladen und Romanzen* (*GW*, 1:184–85).

COMMENTS: no period at end of line 4.

[6] Mignons Lied (Louis Spohr)

Kennst du das Land? wo die Zitronen blühn,	Do you know the land where the lemons grow?
Im dunkeln Laub die Gold-Orangen glühn,	Within dark foliage the golden oranges glow;
Ein sanfter Wind vom blauen Himmel weht,	A gentle breeze blows from the blue heaven;
Die Myrte still und hoch der Lorbeer steht.	Myrtle stands still and the laurel tall.
Kennst du es wohl?	(5) Do you know it?
Dahin! dahin!	There! There
Möcht' ich mit dir, o mein Geliebter ziehn.	Would I go with you, oh my beloved.
Kennst du das Haus? auf Säulen ruht sein Dach,	Do you know the house? Upon pillars rests its roof;
Es glänzt der Saal, es schimmert das Gemach,	The hall glistens, the chamber glimmers,
Und Marmorbilder stehn und sehn mich an:	(10) And marble figures stand and look upon me.
Was hat man dir du armes Kind getan?	What have they done to you, you poor child?

Kennst du es wohl?	Do you know it?
Dahin! dahin!	There! There
Möcht' ich mit dir, o mein Beschützer ziehn.	Would I go with you, oh my guardian!
Kennst du den Berg und seinen Wolkensteg?	(15) Do you know the hill and its beclouded path?
Das Maulthier sucht' im Nebel seinen Weg,	The mule seeks its way in the mist.
In Höhlen wohnt der Drachen alte Brut,	In caves dwell an old brood of dragons.
Es stürzt der Fels und über ihn die Fluth!	The rock plummets and over it the flood.
Kennst du ihn wohl?	Do you know it?
Dahin! dahin!	(20) There! There
Geht unser Weg! o Vater, laß uns ziehn!	Goes our way; oh father, let us go!

    SOURCE OF TEXT: "Kennst du das Land, wo die Citronen blühn," from *Wilhelm Meisters Lehrjahre*, book III, Ch. 1: Mignon's song to Wilhelm (accompanied in the novel by a zither) in *Wilhelm Meisters Theatralische Sendungen*, vol. 4, 1783 (*GW*, 21:233).

[7] *Der Fischer (Moritz Hauptmann)*

Das Wasser rauscht', das Wasser schwoll,	The water rushed, the water swelled,
Ein Fischer saß daran,	A fisherman sat beside it,
Sah nach der Angel ruhevoll,	Looking at the line peacefully,
Kühl bis ans Herz hinan.	Calm through to his heart.
Und wie er sitzt und wie er lauscht,	(5) And as he sits and as he listens,
Teilt sich die Flut empor;	The rising waters divide;
Aus dem bewegten Wasser rauscht	From the rustling water rushes forth
Ein feuchtes Weib hervor.	A water woman.
Sie sang zu ihm, sie sprach zu ihm:	She sang to him, she spoke to him:
Was lockst du meine Brut,	(10) Why do you lure my brood
Mit Menschenwitz und Menschenlist,	With human wit and human ruse
Hinauf in Todesglut?	Up to the fire of death?
Ach! wüßtest du, wie's Fischlein ist	Ah if only you knew, how the little fish is
So wohlig auf dem Grund,	So cozy at the bottom,
Du stiegst herunter wie du bist,	(15) You would climb down there as you are,
Und würdest erst gesund.	And would be well for once.
Labt sich die liebe Sonne nicht,	Do not the lovely sun,
Der Mond sich nicht im Meer?	And the moon, refresh themselves in the sea?
Kehrt wellenatmend ihr Gesicht	Do not their faces turn, breathing waves,
Nicht doppelt schöner her?	(20) Doubly fair?
Lockt dich der tiefe Himmel nicht,	Are you not lured by the deep sky,
Das feuchtverklärte Blau?	By the radiantly moist blue?
Lockt dich dein eigen Angesicht	Are you not lured by your own countenance
Nicht her in ew'gen Tau?	To the eternal dew?
Das Wasser rauscht', das Wasser schwoll,	(25) The water rushed, the water swelled,
Netzt' ihm den nackten Fuß;	Wetting his bare foot;
Sein Herz wuchs ihm so sehnsuchtsvoll,	His heart became so longing,
Wie bei der Liebsten Gruß.	As with the greeting of a beloved.
Sie sprach zu ihm, sie sang zu ihm;	She spoke to him, she sang to him;
Da war's um ihn geschehn:	(30) Then it happened to him:
Halb zog sie ihn, halb sank er hin,	She pulled partly, partly he sank himself,
Und ward nicht mehr gesehn.	And was never again seen.

    SOURCE OF TEXT: "Das Wasser rauscht', das Wasser schwoll," from *Volks- und andere Lieder*, vol. 1 (Weimar, 1779) where it was set to music by S. Freiherr von Seckendorff; and Herder's *Volkslieder*, 1779, as "Das Lied vom Fischer" (*GW*, 1:169–70).

[8] *Der Erlkönig (Bernhard Klein)*

Wer reitet so spät durch Nacht und Wind?—	Who rides so late through night and wind?
Es ist der Vater mit seinem Kind,	It is the father with his child.
Er hat den Knaben wohl in dem Arm,	He has the boy safely in his arm;
Er faßt ihn sicher, er hält ihn warm.	He holds him securely, he keeps him warm.

Mein Sohn, was birgst du so bang dein Gesicht?—	(5) My son, why do you hide your face so worriedly?—
Siehst Vater du den Erlkönig nicht?	Father, do you not see the Erlking?
Den Erlenkönig mit Kron und Schweif?—	The Erlking with crown and train?—
Mein Sohn, es ist ein Nebelstreif.—	My son, it is a streak of fog.—
"Komm liebes Kind, komm geh mit mir!	"You lovely child, come, go with me!
Gar schöne Spiele spiel' ich mit dir;	(10) I shall play quite wonderful games with you;
Manch' bunte Blumen sind an dem Strand,	Many colorful flowers are on the shore;
Meine Mutter hat manch' gülden Gewand."—	My mother has many golden garments."
Mein Vater, mein Vater, und hörest du nicht,	My father, my father, and do you not hear,
Was Erlenkönig mir leise verspricht?—	What Erlking softly promises me?—
Sei ruhig, bleibe ruhig, mein Kind;	(15) Be quiet, stay quiet, my child;
In dürren Blättern säuselt der Wind.—	The wind whispers among the dry leaves.—
"Willst feiner Knabe du mit mir gehn,	"Will you, fine boy, go with me?
Meine Töchter sollen dich warten schön,	My daughters shall wait upon you well;
Meine Töchter führen den nächtlichen Reihn,	My daughters lead the nightly procession,
Und wiegen und tanzen und singen dich ein."—	(20) And shall rock and dance and sing you to sleep."
Mein Vater, mein Vater und siehst du nicht dort,	My father, my father, and do you not see there
Erlkönigs Töchter am düstern Ort?—	Erlking's daughters in that gloomy spot?—
Mein Sohn, mein Sohn ich seh' es genau,	My son, my son, I see it clearly;
Es scheinen die alten Weiden so grau.—	The old willows shine quite grey.—
"Ich lieb' dich, mich reitzt deine schöne Gestalt	(25) "I love you, your lovely figure stirs me;
Und bist du nicht willig, so brauch' ich Gewalt."—	And if you are not willing, then I shall use force."
Mein Vater, mein Vater jetzt faßt er mich an!	My father, my father, he is seizing me now!
Erlkönig hat mir ein Leids getan!	Erlking has caused me pain!—
Dem Vater grauset's, er reitet geschwind,	The father shudders; he rides swiftly.
Und hält in den Armen das ächzende Kind,	(30) He holds in his arms the moaning child.
Erreicht den Hof, mit Müh und Not,	He reaches the town with trouble and stress;
In seinen Armen das Kind war tot.	In his arms the child was dead.

SOURCE OF TEXT: "Wer reitet so spät," first published in the singspiel of 1782, *Die Fischerin*, as the opening ballad (*GW*, 1:167–68).

COMMENTS: line 12, comma after "hat"; line 25, second word is "liebe".

[9] *Der König von Thule* (Heinrich Marschner)

Es war ein König in Thule	There was once a king in Thule
Gar treu bis an das Grab,	Quite loyal unto the grave,
Dem sterbend seine Buhle	To whom his dying mistress
Einen goldnen Becher gab.	A golden goblet gave.
Es ging ihm nichts darüber,	(5) Nothing did he cherish more,
Er leert' ihn jeden Schmaus;	He emptied it at each feast;
Die Augen gingen ihm über,	His eyes filled with tears,
So oft er trank daraus.	Whenever he drank from it.
Und als er kam zu sterben,	And when he came to die,
Zählt' er seine Städt' im Reich,	(10) He counted the towns of the kingdom,
Gönnt' alles seinen Erben,	Bequeathed all to his heirs,
Den Becher nicht zugleich.	But not the goblet.
Er saß beim Königsmahle,	He sat at the king's banquet,
Die Ritter um ihm her,	The knights about him,
Auf hohem Väter-saale,	(15) In the noble hall of the fathers,
Dort auf dem Schloß am Meer.	There at the castle by the sea.
Dort stand der alte Zecher,	There stood the old drinker,
Trank letzte Lebensglut,	Drank the last of life's fervor,
Und warf den heil'gen Becher	And threw the sacred goblet
Hinunter in die Flut.	(20) Down into the tide.
Er sah ihn stürzen, trinken	He saw it fall, drink,
Und sinken tief in's Meer.	And sink deep into the sea.

xxxi

Die Augen täten ihm sinken; His eyes sank closed,
Trank nie einen Tropfen mehr. Never did he drink another drop.

SOURCE OF TEXT: "Es war ein König in Thule," from *Volks- und andere Lieder* (Dessau, 1782), where it was set to music by S. Freiherr von Seckendorff; later in *Faust: Ein Fragment*, 1790, and in *Faust*, part I, 1808 (GW, 14:136).

COMMENTS: line 14, fourth word is "ihn."

[10] Der Zauberlehrling (Carl Loewe)

Hat der alte Hexenmeister	The old sorcerer has
Sich doch einmal wegbegeben	Finally gone away!
Und nun sollen seine Geister	And now his spirits
Auch nach meinem Willen leben	Shall live by my command.
Seine Wort und Werke	(5) His words and deeds
Merkt' ich, und den Brauch,	I noted, and their use,
Und mit Geistes Stärke	And with strength of will
Tu' ich Wunder auch.	I'll work wonders, too.
Walle! walle!	Wander! Wander
Manche Strecke	(10) For some distance,
Daß zum Zwecke	That purposefully
Wasser fließe	The water flows,
Und mit reichem vollen Schwalle	And with teeming full torrent
Zu dem Bade sich ergieße.	Rushes to the pool.
Und nun komm du alter Besen	(15) And now come, you old broom!
Nimm die schlechten Lumpenhüllen,	Take the wretched ragged remains;
Bist schon lange Knecht gewesen	You've been a servant a long time,
Nun erfülle meinen Willen!	Now fulfil my wish!
Auf zwei Beinen stehe,	Stand on two legs,
Oben sei ein Kopf	(20) On top will be your head.
Eile nun und gehe	Hurry now and go
Mit dem Wassertopf.	With your waterpail.
Walle! walle!	Wander! Wander
Manche Strecke	For some distance,
Daß zum Zwecke	(25) That purposefully
Wasser fließe	The water flows,
Und mit reichem vollen Schwalle	And with teeming full torrent
Zu dem Bade sich ergieße.	Rushes to the pool.
Seht er läuft zum Ufer nieder,	Look, he's running to the shore,
Wahrlich! ist schon an dem Flusse!	(30) In fact, he's already by the stream,
Und mit Blitzesschnelle wieder	And with lightning speed once more
Ist er hier mit raschem Gusse	He is here to swiftly pour.
Schon zum zweiten Male!	Again a second time!
Wie das Becken schwillt	How the pail swells!
Wie sich jede Schale	(35) How every bucket
Voll mit Wasser füllt.	Fills with water!
Stehe! stehe!	Stop! Stop!
Denn wir haben	For we have
Deiner Gaben	Your talent
Voll gemessen!	(40) Fully measured!
Ach ich merk' es, wehe! wehe!	Ah, I see it! Woe! Woe!
Hab' ich doch das Wort vergessen.	I've forgotten the word!
Ach das Wort worauf am Ende	Ah, the word, with which at the end
Er das wird was er gewesen,	He will be what he was.
Ach er läuft und bringt behende	(45) Ah, he nimbly runs and fetches!
Wärst du doch der alte Besen!	Were you only the old broom again!
Immer neue Güsse	And other torrents
Bringt er schnell herein	He quickly brings forth,
Ach und hundert Flüsse	Ah, and hundreds of rivers

Stürzen auf mich ein!	(50) Rush at me.
Nein nicht länger	No, no longer
Kann ich's lassen,	Can I bear it;
Will ihn fassen	I'll catch him.
Das ist Tücke!	That is trickery!
Ach nun wird mir immer bänger	(55) Ah, now I am growing more afraid!
Welche Miene welche Blicke!	What a look! What a sight!
O du Ausgeburt der Hölle!	O you child of hell!
Soll das ganze Haus ersaufen?	Will the entire house be drowned?
Seh' ich über jede Schwelle	But over every swell I see
Doch schon Wasserströme laufen	(60) More floods of water rushing.
Du verruchter Besen,	An atrocious broom
Der nicht hören will!	Who will not listen!
Sei der du gewesen	Staff, which you were,
Steh doch wieder still!	Stay still again!
Willst's am Ende	(65) Won't you ever
Gar nicht lassen?	Let it be?
Will dich fassen,	I'll seize you,
Will dich halten	I'll hold you,
Will das alte Holz, behende	And nimbly split the old wood
Mit dem scharfen Beile spalten!	(70) With a sharp axe.
Seht da kommt er schleppend wieder	Look, again he carries more!
Wie ich mich nur auf dich werfe	As I throw myself upon you,
Gleich o Kobold liegst du nieder,	At once, o Cobold, you are down;
Krachend trifft die glatte Schärfe	Noisily the smooth blade strikes.
Wahrlich brav getroffen,	(75) Truly, bravely struck!
Seht er ist entzwei	Look, he is cut in two!
Und nun darf ich hoffen	And now I can hope,
Und ich atme frei!	And I can breathe freely!
Wehe! wehe!	Woe! Woe!
Beide Teile	(80) Both halves
Stehn in Eile	Stand quickly on end
Schon als Knechte	As servants already
Völlig fertig in die Höhe	Fully prepared!
Helft mir, ach! ihr hohen Mächte!	Help me, ah! You almighty forces!
Und sie laufen! naß und nässer	(85) And they run! Wet and wetter
Wird's im Saal und auf den Stufen!	It grows in the hall and on the steps.
Welch entsetzliches Gewässer	What dreadful waters!
Herr und Meister hör mich rufen!	Lord and master! hear my call!
Ach da kommt der Meister	Ah, here comes the master!
Herr die Not ist groß!	(90) Sir, my dismay is great!
Die ich rief die Geister	Those spirits that I called,
Werd' ich nun nicht los,	I now cannot control.
In die Ecke	Into the corner,
Besen! Besen!	Brooms! Brooms!
Seid's gewesen	(95) Be as you were.
Denn als Geister	For as spirits
Ruft euch nur zu seinem Zwecke	You are summoned for his purpose
Erst hervor der alte Meister.	Only by the old master.

    SOURCE OF TEXT: "Hat der alte Hexenmeister," from Schiller's *Musen-Almanach für das Jahr 1798* (GW, 1:215–18).

    COMMENTS: no period at end of line 14; line 81, second word is "im."

[11] *Nähe des Geliebten (Ferdinand Hiller)*
  See [3] for text and translation.

    COMMENTS: line 2, period instead of semicolon; line 6, comma instead of semicolon; line 10, period instead of comma; line 14, last word is "nah"; line 15, comma after "sinkt."

[12] *Wonne der Wehmut (Robert Franz)*

Trocknet nicht, trocknet nicht,	Dry not, dry not,
Tränen der ewigen Liebe!	Tears of eternal love!
Ach! nur dem halbgetrockneten Auge	Ah, only to the half-dry eye
Wie öde wie tot die Welt ihm erscheint!	How desolate, how dead the world appears!
Trocknet nicht, trocknet nicht,	(5) Dry not, dry not,
Tränen unglücklicher Liebe!	Tears of unhappy love!

SOURCE OF TEXT: "Trocknet nicht," from J. F. Reichardt's *Deutsche Gesänge*, 1788 (*GW*, 1:1–97).

[13] *Clärchens Lied (Anton Rubinstein)*

Freudvoll	Joyful
Und leidvoll,	And sorrowful,
Gedankenvoll sein,	Thoughtful to be,
Hangen	Yearning
Und bangen	(5) And worrying
In schwebender Pein,	In lingering pain,
Himmelhoch jauchzend,	Heavenly jubilant,
Zum Tode betrübt,	Deathly despairing,
Glücklich allein	Happy alone
Ist die Seele die liebt!	(10) Is the soul in love.

SOURCE OF TEXT: "Freudvoll," from *Egmont*, in *Goethes Schriften*, 8 vols. (Leipzig: Göschen, 1787–90), vol. 5 (*GW*, 8:237).

[14] *Freisinn (Hans von Bülow)*

Laßt mich nur auf meinem Sattel gelten!	Let me be judged only in my saddle!
Bleibt in euren Hütten, euren Zelten!	You can stay in your huts, your tents!
Und ich reite froh in alle Ferne,	And I shall ride joyfully into the great beyond,
Über meiner Mütze nur die Sterne!	Over my cap only the stars.
Er hat euch die Gestirne gesetzt,	(5) He has created the constellations for you,
Als Leiter zu Land und See,	As guide on land and sea,
Damit ihr euch daran ergötzt,	So that you should be amused,
Stets blickend in die Höh.	Ever gazing on high.

SOURCE OF TEXT: "Laßt mich nur auf meinem Sattel gelten!," from *West-östlicher Divan von Göthe* (Stuttgart: Cotta, 1819) (*GW*, 6:9).

[15] *Nachtgesang (Joseph Rheinberger)*

O! gib vom weichen Pfühle	Oh give me, from the soft cushion,
Träumend ein halb' Gehör!	Dreaming, half an ear!
Bei meinem Saitenspiele	To my stringed music
Schlafe, was willst du mehr?	Sleep! What more could you want?
Bei meinem Saitenspiele	(5) With my stringed music
Segnet der Sterne Heer	The host of stars blesses
Die ewigen Gefühle.	The eternal feelings;
Schlafe, was willst du mehr?	Sleep! What more could you want?
Die ewigen Gefühle	The eternal feelings
Heben mich hoch und hehr	(10) Exalt me, high and mighty,
Aus irdischem Gewühle,	From the mundane crowd;
Schlafe, was willst du mehr?	Sleep! What more could you want?
Vom irdischen Gewühle	From the mundane crowd
Trennst du mich nur zu sehr,	You part me only too well.
Bannst mich in diese Kühle;	(15) You enchant me in this chill;
Schlafe, was willst du mehr?	Sleep! What more could you want?
Bannst mich in diese Kühle,	You enchant me in this chill,
Gibst nur im Traum Gehör!	You listen only in a dream.

Ach! auf dem weichen Pfühle	Ah, on the soft cushion
Schlafe, was willst du mehr?	(20) Sleep! What more could you want?

SOURCE OF TEXT: "O! gib vom weichen Pfühle," from *Taschenbuch auf das Jahr 1804*. The text was based on Reichardt's setting of the Italian folksong *Tu sei quel dolce fuoco* (GW, 1:88).

[16] *Wer sich der Einsamkeit ergibt (Arnold Mendelssohn)*

Wer sich der Einsamkeit ergibt,	He who surrenders to loneliness,
Ach! der ist bald allein,	Ah, he is soon alone;
Ein Jeder lebt, ein Jeder liebt	Another lives, another loves,
Und läßt ihn seiner Pein.	And leaves him to his pain.
Ja laßt mich meiner Qual	(5) Yes! Leave me to my agony!
Und kann ich nur einmal	And if I could but once
Recht einsam sein,	Truly be lonely,
Dann bin ich nicht allein.	Then I'll not be alone.
Es schleicht ein Liebender lauschend sacht,	A lover creeps softly to eavesdrop;
Ob seine Freundin allein,	(10) Is his beloved alone?
So über schleicht bei Tag und Nacht	So by day and night
Mich Einsamen die Pein,	Pain overcomes lonely me,
Mich Einsamen die Qual.	Agony overcomes lonely me.
Ach werd' ich erst einmal,	Ah I shall only be
Einsam im Grabe sein,	(15) Lonely in the grave,
Da laßt sie mich allein.	Then it will leave me alone!

SOURCE OF TEXT: "Wer sich der Eisamkeit ergibt," from *Wilhelm Meisters Theatralische Sendungen*, vol. 4, 1783 (GW, 21:219–20).

[17] *Am Flusse (Arnold Mendelssohn)*

Verfließet, vielgeliebte Lieder,	Flow away, most beloved songs,
Zum Meere der Vergessenheit!	To the sea of oblivion!
Kein Knabe sing' entzückt euch wieder,	No enraptured youth will sing you again,
Kein Mädchen in der Blütenzeit.	Nor maiden at blossom time.
Ihr sanget nur von meiner Lieben;	(5) You sang only of my love;
Nun spricht sie meiner Treue Hohn.	Now she mocks my loyalty.
Ihr wart ins Wasser eingeschrieben,	You were written on water,
So fließt denn auch mit ihm davon.	So flow then away with it.

SOURCE OF TEXT: "Verfließt, vielgeliebte Lieder," from Schiller's *Musen-Almanach für das Jahr 1799* (GW, 1:61).

[18] *Lied des Mephistopheles (Ferruccio Busoni)*

Es war einmal ein König,	Once upon a time there was a king
Der hatt' einen großen Floh,	Who had a great flea
Den liebt' er gar nicht wenig,	Whom he loved not a little,
Als wie seinen eigenen Sohn.	As if it were his own son.
Da rief er seinen Schneider,	(5) Once he called to his tailor;
Der Schneider kam heran:	The tailor came forth.
Da, miß dem Junker Kleider	Now, measure clothes for the squire,
Und miß ihm Hosen an.	And measure trousers for him!
In Sammet und in Seide	In velvet and in silk
War er nun angetan,	(10) He was now attired,
Hatte Bänder auf dem Kleide,	Had ribbons on his clothes,
Hatt' auch ein Kreuz daran,	Had a cross on them, too,
Und war sogleich Minister	And was at once a minister,
Und hatt einen großen Stern.	And had a large star.
Da wurden seine Geschwister	(15) Now his brothers and sisters became
Bei Hof auch große Herrn.	Grand people at the court, too.

Und Herrn und Fraun am Hofe,	And the lords and ladies of the court
Die warn' sehr geplagt,	Were very tormented.
Die Kön'gin und die Zofe	The queen and her maid
Gestochen und genagt,	(20) Were bitten and gnawed,
Und durften sie nicht knicken	And could not slap them
Und weg sie jucken nicht.	And scratch them away.
Wir knicken und ersticken	We slap and smother them
Doch gleich, wenn einer sticht.	Nevertheless whenever one bites.

> SOURCE OF TEXT: "Es war einmal ein König," from *Faust: Ein Fragment*, 1790, later in *Faust*, part I, 1808 (*GW*, 14:105–6). Auerbach's Cellar; Mephistopheles' song of the flea. In the source, the first and second strophes are interrupted by four lines from Brander, and at the conclusion the final two lines of the third strophe are repeated by a jubilant chorus.

[19] *Mailied (Hans Pfitzner)*

Wie herrlich leuchtet	How lovely shines
Mir die Natur!	Nature to me!
Wie glänzt die Sonne!	How the sun gleams!
Wie lacht die Flur!	How the field laughs!
Es dringen Blüten	(5) Blossoms burst
Aus jedem Zweig	From every branch
Und tausend Stimmen	And a thousand voices
Aus dem Gesträuch.	From the brushes.
Und Freud' und Wonne	And pleasure and delight
Aus jeder Brust.	(10) From every breast.
O Erd', o Sonne!	O earth, O sun!
O Glück, o Lust!	O joy, O happiness!
O Lieb', o Liebe!	O love, O love!
So golden schön,	So beautifully golden,
Wie Morgenwolken	(15) Like morning clouds
Auf jenen Höh'n!	On distant summits!
Du segnest herrlich	You gloriously bless
Das frische Feld,	The fresh field
Im Blütendampfe	In scent of blossoms
Die volle Welt.	(20) The whole world.
O Mädchen, Mädchen,	O maiden, maiden,
Wie lieb' ich dich!	How I love you!
Wie blinkt dein Auge!	How your eyes appear!
Wie liebst du mich!	How you love me!
So liebt die Lerche	(25) As the lark loves
Gesang und Luft,	Song and air,
Und Morgenblumen	And morning blossoms,
Den Himmelsduft,	Heaven's fragrance,
Wie ich dich liebe	So do I love you
Mit warmem Blut,	(30) With passionate blood.
Die du mir Jugend	You give me youth
Und Freud' und Mut	And joy and courage
Zu neuen Liedern	For new songs
Und Tänzen gibst.	And dances.
Sei ewig glücklich,	(35) Be forever happy,
Wie du mich liebst!	As you love me!

> SOURCE OF TEXT: "Wie herrlich leuchtet," from *Iris* 2, no. 6 (1775): 75–77, under the title *Maifest* (*GW*, 1:72–73).

> COMMENTS: line 8, comma at end of line; line 13, second word is "Lieb"; line 30, second word is "warmen."

[20] *An den Mond (Justus Hermann Wetzel)*

Füllest wieder Busch und Tal	Fill again thicket and valley
Still mit Nebelglanz,	Still with foggy luster,
Lösest endlich auch einmal	And release at last
Meine Seele ganz.	My soul completely.
Breitest über mein Gefild	(5) Spread over my fields
Lindernd deinen Blick,	Your soothing glance,
Wie des Freundes Auge mild	Like a friend's gentle eye
Über mein Geschick.	Over my fate.
Jeden Nachklang fühlt mein Herz	My heart feels each echo
Froh—und trüber Zeit,	(10) Of a gay—and dreary—time.
Wandle zwischen Freud und Schmerz	Changing between joy and pain
In der Einsamkeit.	In loneliness.
Fließe, fließe, lieber Fluß!	Flow on, flow on beloved river!
Nimmer werd' ich froh,	Never shall I be happy.
So verrauschte Scherz und Kuß,	(15) Thus did jest and kiss vanish,
Und die Treue so.	And faithfulness, too.
Ich besaß es doch einmal,	But I had it once,
Was so köstlich ist!	What so precious is!
Daß man doch zu seiner Qual	That we though tormented
Nimmer es vergißt!	(20) Never forget!
Rausche, Fluß, das Tal entlang,	Rustle on, river, through the valley,
Ohne Rast und Ruh,	Without pause or rest;
Rausche, flüstre meinem Sang	Rustle on, whisper to my song
Melodien zu,	Melodies,
Wenn du in der Winternacht	(25) When in the winter's night you
Wütend überschwillst,	Overflow enraged,
Oder um die Frühlingspracht	Or in the splendor of spring
Junger Knospen quillst.	Drench young buds.
Selig, wer sich vor der Welt	Blessed is he who from the world
Ohne Haß verschließt,	(30) Withdraws without hatred,
Einen Freund am Busen hält	Holds a friend to his heart
Und mit dem genießt,	And with him enjoys,
Was von Menschen nicht gewußt	What is not known by men
Oder nicht bedacht,	Or not considered.
Durch das Labyrinth der Brust	(35) Through the labyrinth of the breast
Wandelt in der Nacht.	Wander in the night.

SOURCE OF TEXT: "Füllest wieder Busch und Tal," from *Goethes Schriften*, vol. 8, *Gedichte* (Leipzig: Goschen, 1789) (GW, 1·100–1)

[21] *Geweihter Platz (Nikolay Karlovich Medtner)*

Wenn zu den Reihen der Nymphen versammelt in heiliger Mondnacht	When among the ranks of the Nymphs, assembled in the holy moonlight,
Sich die Grazien heimlich herab vom Olympus gesellen	Mingle the graces, descended secretly from Olympus,
Hier belauscht sie der Dichter und hört die schönen Gesänge	Here the poet overhears them and listens to the lovely songs,
Sieht verschwiegener Tänze geheimnißvolle Bewegung.	Sees the silent dances, the secret movements.
Was der Himmel nur herrliches hat was glücklich die Erde	(5) What in heaven is wonderful, what the earth with joy
Reizendes immer gebar. Das erscheint dem wachenden Träumer.	Brings forth always, this appears to the awakened dreamer.
Alles erzählt er den Musen und daß die Götter nicht zürnen	He relates all to the muses, and so as not to offend the Gods,

Lehren die Musen ihn gleich bescheiden	The muses humbly instruct him in the mysteries.
Geheimnisse sprechen.	

SOURCE OF TEXT: "Wenn zu den Reihen der Nymphen," from *Goethes Schriften*, vol. 8, *Gedichte* (Leipzig: Göschen, 1789) (GW, 2:128).

[22] *Rastlose Liebe (Othmar Schoeck)*

Dem Schnee, dem Regen,	Through snow and rain,
Dem Wind entgegen,	Against the wind,
Im Dampf der Klüfte,	In the mist of cliffs,
Durch Nebeldüfte,	Through thick fog,
Immer zu! Immer zu!	(5) Forever onward, forever onward!
Ohne Rast und Ruh!	Without rest and peace!
Lieber durch Leiden	Rather through grief
Möcht' ich mich schlagen,	Would I persist,
Als so viel Freuden	Than so many joys
Des Lebens ertragen.	(10) Of life bear.
Alle das Neigen	All the longing,
Von Herzen zu Herzen,	From heart to heart,
Ach, wie so eigen	Ah, how strangely
Schaffet das Schmerzen!	It causes pain!
Wie soll ich fliehen?	(15) How can I escape?
Wälderwärts ziehen?	Toward the woods?
Alles vergebens!	All is in vain!
Krone des Lebens,	Crown of life,
Glück ohne Ruh,	Joy without rest,
Liebe, bist du!	(20) Beloved, are you!

SOURCE OF TEXT: "Dem Schnee, dem Regen," from *Goethes Schriften*, vol. 8, *Gedichte* (Leipzig: Göschen, 1789) (GW, 1:84).

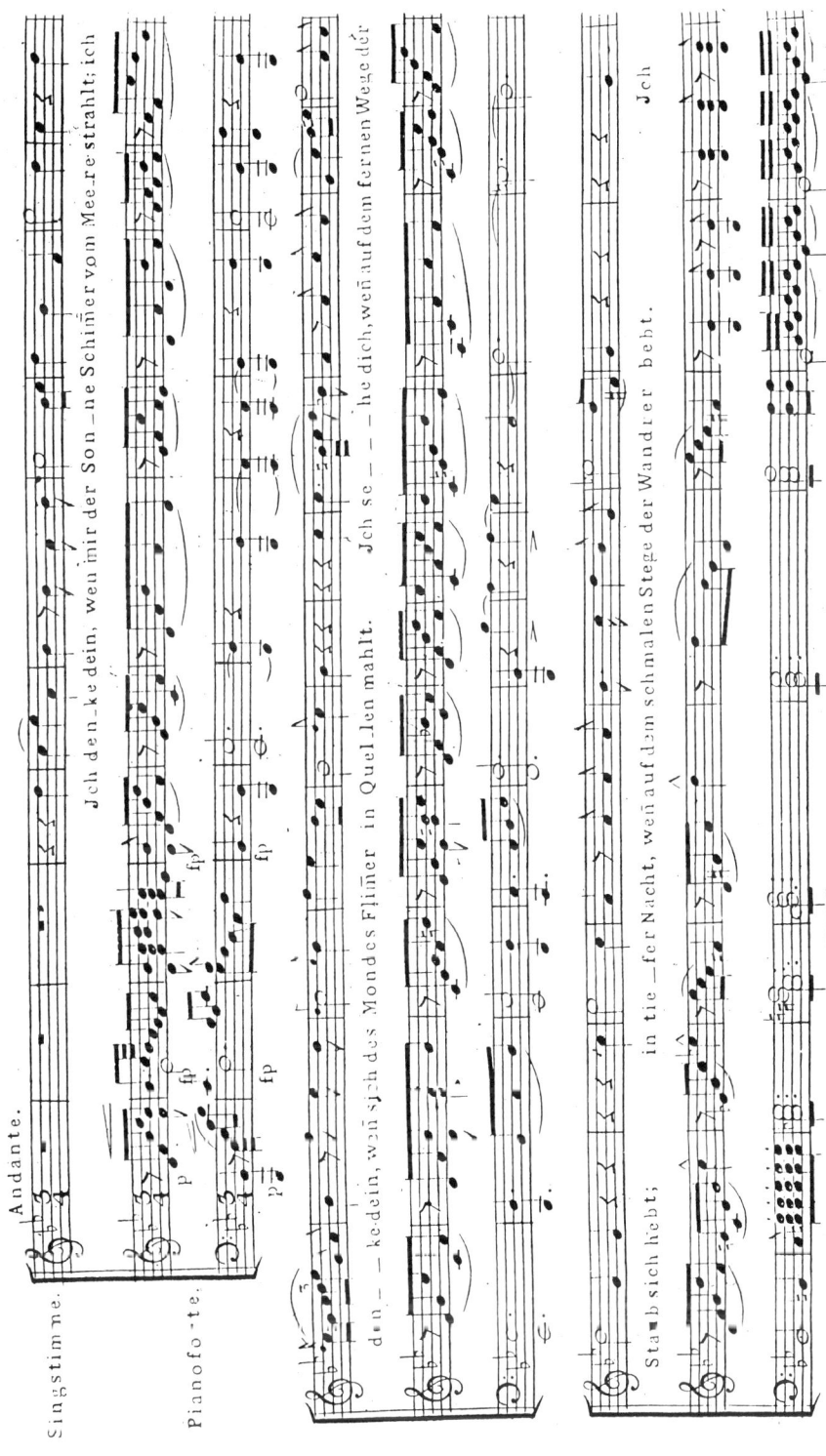

Plate 1. Wenzel Johann Tomaschek, first page of *Nähe des Geliebten* ([3] in this anthology), published by Marco Berra in Prague, 1815. Reprinted by permission of the University of California, Berkeley, Music Library.

Plate 2. Bernhard Klein, first page of *Der Erlkönig* ([8] in this anthology), published by N. Simrock in Bonn, 1827. Reprinted by permission of the William A. Speck Collection of Goetheana, Yale University Library.

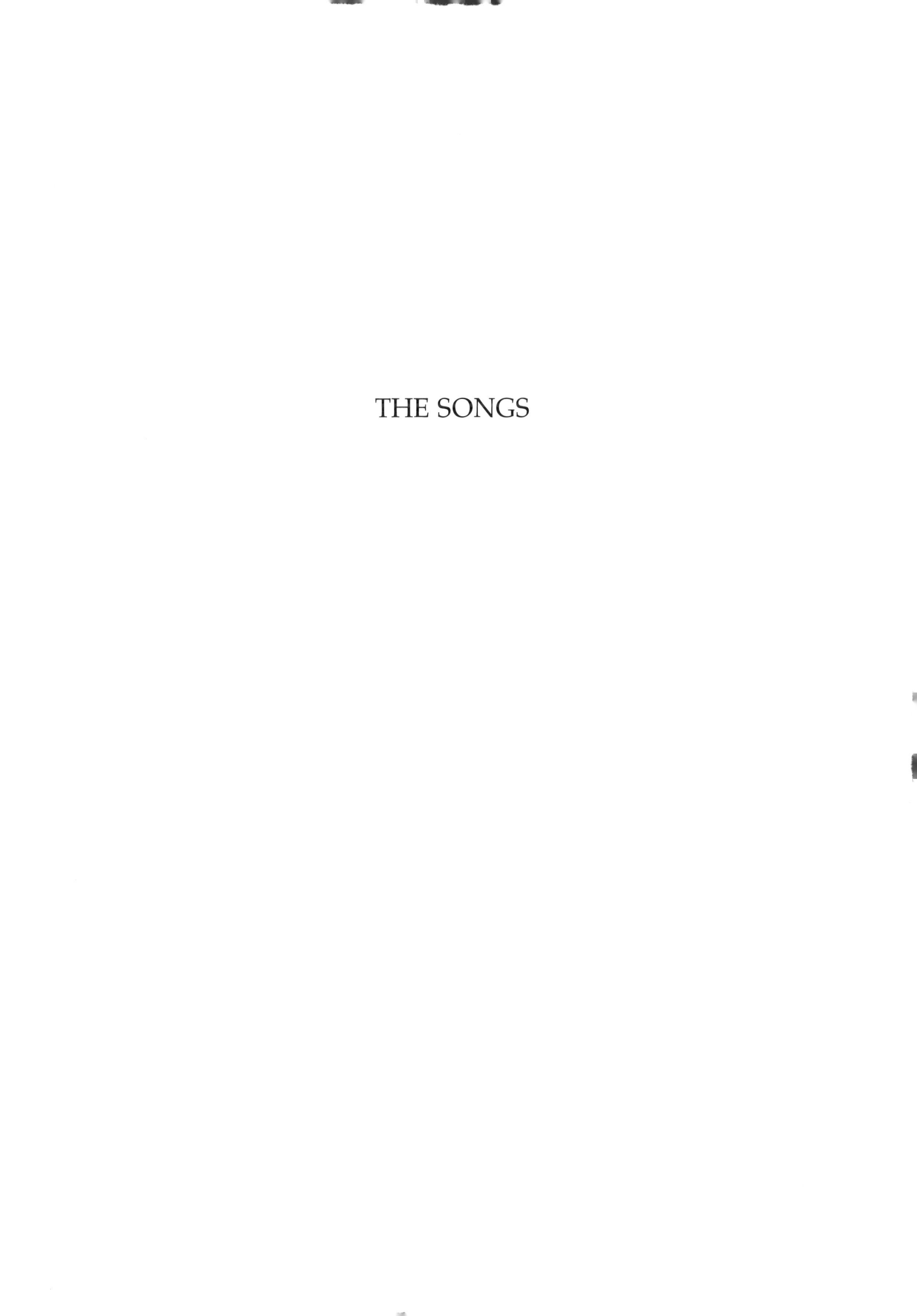

THE SONGS

[1] Sehnsucht

Carl Zelter

Nur wer die Sehnsucht kennt, Weiß, was ich leide! Allein und abgetrennt Von aller Freude, Seh' ich an's Firmament Nach jener Seite. Ach, der mich liebt ___ und kennt, Ist in der Wei- te. Es schwin- det

zunehmend *nachlassend*

mir, es brennt Mein Ein- ge- wei- de. Nur wer die Sehn- sucht kennt, Weiß,

[*zunehmend*] [*nachlassend*]

was ich lei- de!

[2] Das Blümlein Wunderschön
Lied des gefangenen Grafen

Johann Rudolf Zumsteeg

Mäßig Langsam

[1. *Graf*] Ich kenn' ein Blüm-lein Wun-der-schön Und tra-ge dar-nach Ver-lan-gen, Ich möcht' es ger-ne zu su-chen gehn, Al-lein ich bin ge-fan-gen; Die Schmer-zen sind mir nicht ge-ring, Denn als ich in der Frei-heit ging, Da hatt' ich es in der Nä-he.

[2.]
Von diesem ringsum steilen Schloß
Lass ich die Augen schweifen,
Und kann's vom hohen Thurmgeschoß
Mit Blicken nicht ergreifen,
Und wer mir's vor die Augen brächt,
Er wäre Ritter oder Knecht,
Der sollte mein Trauter bleiben.

[3.] *Rose* Ich blü- he schön und hö- re dies, Hier un- ter dei- nem Git- ter, Du mein- est mich, die Ro- se, ge- wiß Du edler armer Ritter. Du hast gar einen hohen Sinn, Es herrscht die Blumenkönigin Gewiß auch in deinem Herzen.

Es ist zu bemerken, dass das, was die Lilie, die Nelke und das Veilchen sagen, nach der Melodie der Rose, im Zweiviertheil-Takt gesungen wird; der Graf hingegen bleibt immer bei der ersten Melodie. Die kleinen Veränderungen, dass hie und da aus einer Note Zwei, oder aus zwei Eine gemacht werden muss, geben sich von selbst, wie z. B. gleich in der folgenden Strophe.

(It should be noted that the texts of the lily, the carnation, and the violet are to be sung to the melody of the rose, in $\frac{2}{4}$ meter; the count, however, retains the first melody. The small changes that must be made here and there from one note to two or from two notes to one are to be expected, as, for example, in the following strophe.)

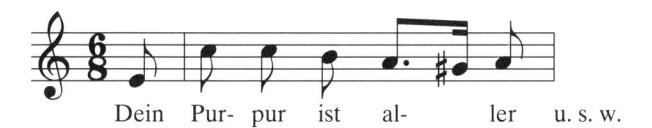

Dein Pur- pur ist al- ler u. s. w.

[4.]
Graf
Dein Purpur ist aller Ehren wert,
Im grünen Überkleide,
Darob das Mädchen dein begehrt,
Wie Gold und Edelgeschmeide.
Dein Kranz erhöht das schönste Gesicht,
Allein du bist das Blümchen nicht
Das ich im Stillen verehre.

[5.]
Lilie
Das Röschen hat gar stolzen Brauch
Und strebet immer nach oben,
Doch wird ein liebes Liebchen auch
Der Lilie Zierde loben.
Wenn's Herze schlägt in treuer Brust,
Und ist sich rein, wie ich, bewußt,
Der hält mich wohl am höchsten.

[6.]
Graf
Ich nenne mich zwar keusch und rein
Und rein von bösen Fehlen,
Doch muß ich hier gefangen sein
Und muß mich einsam quälen.
Du bist mir zwar ein schönes Bild
Von mancher Jungfrau rein und mild,
Doch weiß ich noch 'was Liebers.

[7.]
Nelke
Das mag wohl ich die Nelke sein,
Hier in des Wächters Garten,
Wie würde sonst der Alte mein
Mit so viel Sorge warten?
Im schönen Kreis der Blätter Drang,
Und Wohlgeruch das Leben lang,
Und alle tausend Farben.

[8.]
Graf
Die Nelke soll man nicht verschmähn,
Sie ist des Gärtners Wonne,
Bald muß sie in dem Lichte stehn,
Bald schützt er sie vor Sonne,
Doch was den Grafen glücklich macht
Es ist nicht ausgesuchte Pracht,
Es ist ein stilles Blümchen.

[9.]
Veilchen
Ich steh' verborgen und gebückt,
Und mag nicht gerne sprechen,
Doch will ich, weil sich's eben schickt,
Mein tiefes Schweigen brechen,
Wenn ich es bin, du guter Mann,
Wie schmerzt mich's daß ich hinauf nicht kann,
Dir alle Gerüche senden.

[10.]
Graf
Das gute Veilchen schätz' ich sehr,
Es ist so gar bescheiden,
Und duftet so schön, doch brauch' ich mehr
In meinen herben Leiden,
Ich will es euch nur eingestehn
Auf diesen dürren Felsenhöh'n
Ist's Liebchen nicht zu finden.

[11.]
Doch wandelt unten an dem Bach
Das treuste Weib der Erde,
Und seufzet leise manches Ach,
Bis ich erlöset werde.
Wenn sie ein blaues Blümchen bricht
Und immer sagt: Vergiß mein nicht!
So fühl' ich's in der Ferne.

[12.]
Ja in der Ferne fühlt sich die Macht
Wenn zwei sich redlich lieben,
D'rum bin ich in des Kerkers Nacht
Auch noch lebendig geblieben,
Und wenn mir fast das Herze bricht,
So ruf' ich nur: Vergiß mein nicht!
Da komm' ich wieder ins Leben.

[3] Nähe des Geliebten

Wenzel Johann Tomaschek

Andante ♩ = 60

Ich den- ke dein, wenn mir der Son- ne Schim- mer Vom Mee- re strahlt; Ich den- ke dein, wenn sich des Mon- des Flim- mer In Quel- len malt. Ich se- he dich, wenn auf dem fer- nen__ We- ge Der Staub sich hebt;

In tie- fer Nacht, wenn auf dem schma- len Ste- ge der Wand- rer__ bebt. Ich hö- re

dich, wenn dort mit dump- fem Rau- schen Die Wel- le steigt. Im stil- len Hai- ne geh' ich oft zu lau- schen, Wenn al- les schweigt. Ich bin — bei dir, du seist auch noch so — fer- ne, Du bist mir nah'! Die Son- ne — sinkt, bald leuch- ten — mir die Ster- ne. O wärst du da! O wärst — du — da! O wärst du da!

[4] Das Veilchen

Wenzel Johann Tomaschek

Andante ♩ = 66

Ein Veil- chen auf der Wie- se stand, Ge- bückt in sich und un- be- kannt; Es war ein her- zig's Veil- chen. Da kam ei- ne jun- ge

*auch für eine Bass-Stimme geeignet (may also be sung by a bass voice)

Schä-fer-in, Mit leich-tem Schritt und mun-term Sinn, Da- her, da- her, Die Wie- se her, und sang.

Ach! denkt das Veil-chen, wär' ich nur Die schön-ste Blu- me der Na- tur, Ach, nur ein klei-nes Weil-chen, Bis mich das Lieb- chen ab- ge-pflückt, Und an dem Bu- sen matt ge-drückt! Ach

nur, ach nur, Ein Vier- tel- stünd- chen lang!

Ach! a- ber ach! das Mäd- chen kam, Und nicht in

acht das Veil- chen nahm, Er- trat das ar- me Veil- chen. Es sank und starb und freut' sich noch: Und sterb' ich denn, so sterb' ich doch Durch sie, durch sie, zu ihren Füßen doch.

[5] Die Spinnerin

Ferdinand Ries

Mäßig

[1.] Als ich still und ruhig spann Ohne nur zu stocken Trat ein schöner junger Mann Nahe mir zum Rocken. Lobte was zu loben war, Konnte das was schaden? Mein dem Flachse glei- ches Haar, Und den glei- chen Fa- den.

2.
Ruhig war er nicht dabei
Ließ es nicht beim Alten;
Und der Faden riß entzwei,
Den ich lang erhalten.
Und des Flachses Stein-Gewicht,
Gab noch viele Zahlen;
Aber ach! ich konnte nicht
Mehr mit ihnen prahlen.

3.
Als ich sie zum Weber trug,
Fühlt' ich was sich regen,
Und mein armes Herze schlug
Mit geschwindern Schlägen.
Nun beim heißen Sonnenstich,
Bring' ich's auf die Bleiche
Und mit Mühe bück' ich mich
Nach dem nächsten Teiche.

4. Was ich in dem Käm- mer- lein, Still und fein ges-

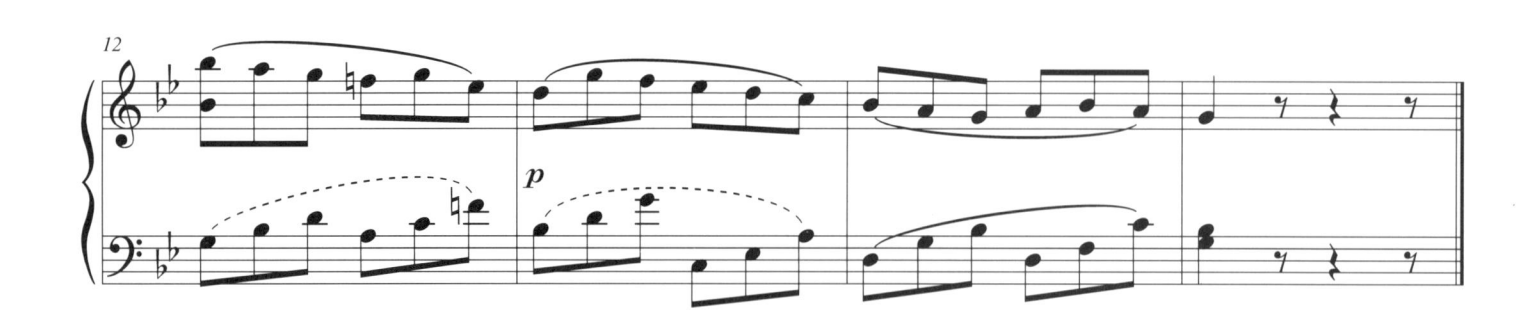

-pon- nen, Kommt, wie kann es an- ders sein? End- lich an die Son- nen, End- lich an die Son- nen.

cresc.

p

[6] Mignons Lied

Louis Spohr

Feierlich

Kennst du das Land? wo die Zi- tro- nen blühn, Im dun- keln Laub die Gold-O- ran- gen glühn, Ein sanf- ter Wind vom blau- en Him- mel weht, Die Myr- te still und hoch der Lor- beer steht. Kennst du es wohl? Da- -hin! da- hin! Möcht' ich mit dir, o mein Ge- lieb- ter ziehn. Kennst du das

Haus? auf Säu- len ruht sein Dach, Es glänzt der Saal, es schim-mert das Ge--mach, Und Mar-mor- bil- der stehn und sehn mich an: Was hat man dir du ar- mes Kind ge--tan? Kennst du es wohl? Da- hin! da- hin! Möcht' ich mit dir, o mein Be-schüt- zer ziehn. Kennst du den Berg und sei-nen Wol- ken-

-steg? Das Maul-thier sucht' im Ne- bel sei- nen Weg, In Höh- len wohnt der Dra- chen al- te Brut, Es stürzt der Fels und ü-ber ihn die Fluth! Kennst du ihn wohl? Da- hin! da- hin! Geht un-ser Weg! o Va- ter, laß uns ziehn! o Va- ter, laß uns ziehn!

[7] Der Fischer

Moritz Hauptmann

cre- scen- do

cre - scen - do

Das Was- ser rauscht', das

Wasser schwoll, Ein Fischer saß daran, Sah nach der Angel ruhevoll, Kühl bis ans Herz hinan. Und wie er sitzt und wie er lauscht, Teilt sich die Flut empor; Aus dem bewegten Wasser rauscht Ein feuchtes Weib hervor. Sie

sang zu ihm, sie sprach zu ihm: Was lockst du meine Brut, Mit Menschenwitz und Menschenlist, Hinauf in Todesglut? Ach! wüßtest du, wie's Fischlein ist So wohlig auf dem Grund, So

wohlig auf dem Grund, Du stiegst herunter wie du bist, Und würdest erst gesund. Labt sich die liebe Sonne nicht, Der Mond sich nicht im Meer? Kehrt wellenatmend

ihr Ge-sicht Nicht dop- pelt schö- ner her? Lockt dich der tie- fe Him- mel nicht, Das feucht- ver-klär- te Blau? Lockt dich dein ei- gen An- ge-sicht Nicht her in ew'- gen Tau? Der tie- fe Him- mel nicht? Das feucht- ver-klär- te Blau? Nicht her in

ew'- gen Tau? der tie- fe Him- mel nicht? Das

feucht- ver-klär- te Blau? Nicht her in ew'- gen, ew'- gen

Tau?

Das Was- ser rauscht', das

Wasser schwoll, Netzt' ihm den nackten Fuß; Sein Herz wuchs ihm so sehnsuchtsvoll, Wie bei der Liebsten Gruß. Sie sprach zu ihm, sie sang zu ihm; Da war's um ihn ge-

-schehn: Halb zog sie ihn, halb sank er hin, Und ward nicht mehr, nicht mehr ge- sehn.

[8] Der Erlkönig

Bernhard Klein

hält ihn warm. Mein Sohn, was birgst du so bang dein Ge-sicht?— Siehst Va-ter du den Erl- kö- nig nicht? Den Er- len- kö- nig mit Kron und Schweif?— Mein Sohn, es ist ein

Ne- bel- streif.— "Komm lie- bes Kind, komm geh mit mir! Gar schö- ne Spie- le spiel' ich mit dir; Manch' bun- te Blu- men sind an dem Strand, Mei- ne Mut- ter hat manch'

gül- den Ge- wand." — Mein Va- ter, mein Va- ter, und hö- rest du nicht, Was Er- len- kö- nig mir lei- se ver- spricht? — Sei ru- hig, blei- be ru- hig mein Kind; In dür- ren Blät- tern

säuselt der Wind.— "Willst feiner Knabe du mit mir gehn, Meine Töchter sollen dich warten schön, Meine Töchter führen den nächtlichen Reihn, Und wiegen und tanzen und singen dich ein."— Mein Vater, mein Vater und siehst du nicht dort, Erlkönigs Töchter am düstern Ort?— Mein Sohn, mein Sohn ich seh' es genau, Es scheinen die alten Weiden so grau. ["]Ich lieb' dich, mich reitzt deine

37

schö- ne Ge- stalt Und bist du nicht wil- lig, so brauch' ich Ge--walt."
Mein Va- ter, mein Va- ter jetzt faßt er mich

Sehr bewegt
[Sehr bewegt]

Nach und nach langsa - - mer
an! Erl- kö- nig hat mir ein Leids ge- tan!
[Nach und nach langsa - - mer]

In der ersten Bewegung
Dem Va- ter grau- set's, er rei- tet ge-
[In der ersten Bewegung]

38

-schwind, Und hält in den Ar- men das äch- zen- de Kind, Er- reicht den Hof, mit Müh und Not,

Nach und nach langsamer

In sei- nen Ar- men das Kind

[*Nach und nach langsamer*]

war tot.

p

pp

[9] Der König von Thule

Heinrich Marschner

Mäßig bewegt, mit Einfachheit und Ernst

Es war ein König in Thule Gar treu bis an das Grab, Dem sterbend seine Buhle Einen goldnen Becher gab. Es ging ihm nichts darüber, Er leert' ihn jeden Schmaus; Die Augen gingen ihm über, So oft er trank dar-

-aus, Die Au- gen gin-gen ihm ü- ber, So oft er trank dar- aus.

Und als er kam zu sterben, Zählt' er sei- ne Städt' im Reich, Gönnt' al- les sei- nen Er- ben, Den Be- cher nicht zu- gleich. Er saß beim Kö- nigs- mah- le, Die

Rit- ter um ihm her, Auf ho- hem Vä- ter- saa- le, Dort auf dem Schloß am Meer, Auf ho- hem Vä- ter- saa- le, Dort auf dem Schloß, auf dem Schloß am Meer.

Dort stand der al- te Ze- cher, Trank letz- te Le- bens- glut, Und warf den heil'- gen

Be- cher Hin- un- ter in die Flut. Er sah ihn stür- zen, trin- ken Und sin- ken tief in's Meer. Die Au- gen tä- ten ihm sin- ken, Die Au- gen tä- ten ihm sin- ken; Trank nie ei- nen Trop- fen mehr, Trank nie ei- nen Trop- fen mehr.

[10] Der Zauberlehrling

Carl Loewe

Vivacissimo

Hat der alte Hexenmeister Sich doch einmal weggegeben
Und nun sollen seine Geister Auch nach meinem Willen leben
Seine Wort und Werke Merkt' ich, und den Brauch, Und mit Geistes Stärke
Tu' ich Wunder auch. Walle! walle!

Man- che Strek- ke Daß zum Zwek- ke
Was- ser flie- ße Und mit rei- chem vol- len Schwal- le
Zu dem Ba- de sich er- gie- ße. Und nun komm du al- ter Be- sen
Nimm die schlech- ten Lum- pen- hül- len, Bist schon lan- ge Knecht ge- we- sen

Nun er- fül- le mei- nen Wil- len! Auf zwei Bei- nen ste- he, O- ben sei ein Kopf Ei- le nun und ge- he Mit dem Was- ser-topf Wal- le! wal- le! Man- che Strek- ke Daß zum Zwek- ke Was- ser flie- ße

Und mit rei- chem vol- len Schwal- le Zu dem Ba- de sich er- gie- ße.

Seht er läuft zum U- fer nie- der, Wahr- lich! ist schon an dem Flu- ße!

Und mit Blit- zes- schnel- le wie- der Ist er hier mit rasch- em Gu- ße

cresc.

Schon zum zwei- ten Ma- le! Wie das Bek- ken schwillt

Wie sich je- de Scha- le Voll mit Was- ser-füllt.

Ste- he! ste- he! Denn wir ha- ben

Dei- ner Ga- ben Voll ge- mes- sen!

Ach Ich merk' es, we- he! we- he! Hab' Ich doch das Wort ver-ges- sen.

46 *cresc.*

Ach das Wort wor- auf am En- de Er das wird was er ge- we- sen,

48

Ach er läuft und bringt be- hen- de Wärst du doch der al- te Be- sen!

50

Im- mer neu- e Güs- se Bringt er schnell he- rein

52 *f*

Ach und hun- dert Flüs- se Stür- zen auf mich ein!

54

Nein nicht län- ger Kann ich's las- sen,

stacc.

56

Will ihn fas- sen Das ist Tük- ke!

58 *dim.*

Ach nun wird mir im- mer bän- ger Wel- che Mie- ne wel- che Bli- cke!

p

dim.

60 *cresc.*

O du Aus- ge- burt der Höl- le! Soll das gan- ze Haus er- sau- fen?

cresc.

Seh' ich ü- ber je- de Schwel- le Doch schon Was- ser- strö- me lau- fen

Du ver- ruch- ter Be- sen, Der nicht hö- ren will!

Sei der du ge- we- sen Steh doch wie- der still!

Willst's am En- de Gar nicht las- sen?

tenuto

Will dich fas- sen, Will dich hal- ten

Will das al- te Holz, be-hen- de Mit dem schar- fen Bei- le spal- ten!

Seht da kommt er schlep- pend wie- der Wie ich mich nun auf dich wer- fe

Gleich o Ko- bold liegst du nie- der, Kra- chend trifft die glat- te Schär- fe

78
un poco meno allegro
p
ritenuto
Wahr- lich brav ge- trof- fen,
Seht er ist ent-zwei
Und nun darf ich hof- fen
[un poco meno allegro]
p
[ritenuto]
81
a tempo
ff
Und ich at- me frei!
We- he!
f [a tempo]
ff
Ped.
83
stacc.
we- he!
Bei- de Tei- le
85
Stehn in Ei- le
Schon als Knech- te

87
Völ- lig fer- tig in die Hö- he Helft mir, ach! ihr ho- hen Mäch- te!

89 *p*
Und sie lau- fen! naß und näs- ser Wird's im Saal und auf den Stu- fen!

91
Welch ent- setz- li- ches Ge- wäs- *ff* ser

93 *ff*
Herr und Mei- ster hör mich ru- fen!

Ach da kommt der Meister Herr die Not ist groß!
Die ich rief die Geister Werd' ich nun nicht los, In die Ek-ke Besen! Besen! Seid's gewesen Denn als Geister Ruft euch nur zu seinem Zwek-ke Erst hervor der alte Meister.

[11] Nähe des Geliebten

Ferdinand Hiller

Andante espressivo

Ich denke dein, wenn mir der Sonne Schimmer Vom Meere strahlt. Ich denke dein, wenn sich des Mondes Flimmer In Quellen malt.

Ich sehe dich, wenn auf dem fernen Wege Der

Staub sich hebt, In tiefer Nacht, wenn auf dem schmalen Stege

Der Wand-rer bebt. Ich hö- re dich,

wenn dort mit dum- pfem Rau- schen Die Wel- le steigt;

Im stil- len Hai- ne geh' ich oft zu lau- schen, Wenn al- les schweigt.

Ich bin bei dir, du seist auch noch so ferne, Du bist mir nah. Die Sonne sinkt, bald leuchten mir die Sterne. O wärst du da, o wärst du da, wärst du da, o wärst du da!

[12] Wonne der Wehmut

Robert Franz

Larghetto

Trock- net nicht, trock- net nicht, Trä- nen der e- wi- gen Lie- be! Ach! nur dem halb- ge- trock- ne- ten Au- ge Wie ö- de wie tot die Welt ihm er- scheint! Trock- net nicht, trock- net nicht, Trä- nen un- glück- li- cher Lie- be!

[13] Clärchens Lied

Anton Rubinstein

Andante con moto

Freud-voll Und leid-voll, Ge-dan-ken-voll sein, Han-gen Und ban-gen In schwe-ben-der

Pein, Himmel hoch jauchzend,

Zum Tode betrübt,

Glücklich allein Ist die

Seele die liebt, die

See- le die liebt, die

See- le die liebt, die

liebt, die liebt!

[14] Freisinn

Hans von Bülow

Vivace, con brio

Laßt mich nur _____ auf meinem Sattel gelten! Bleibt _____ in euren Hütten, bleibt _____ in euren Zelten, Laßt mich nur, _____ mich nur _____ auf meinem Sattel gelten! Und ich reite froh in alle Ferne, Über meiner Mütze nur die Sterne, Über meiner Mütze nur die Sterne, nur die Sterne!

Er hat euch die Gestirne gesetzt, Als Leiter zu Land und See, Damit ihr euch daran ergötzt, Stets, stets, stets blickend in die Höh. Laßt mich nur auf meinem Sattel gelten! Bleibt in euren Hütten, bleibt in euren Zelten, Laßt, laßt mich nur auf meinem Sattel gelten! Und ich reite froh, froh in alle Ferne, Über meiner Mütze nur, nur die Sterne,

Ü- ber mei- ner Mü- tze nur die Ster- ne, nur _____ die Ster- ne!

[15] Nachtgesang

Joseph Rheinberger

Moderato, sempre sotto voce

1. O! gib vom weichen Pfühle
   Träumend ein halb' Gehör!
   Bei meinem Saitenspiele
   Schlafe, was willst du mehr,
   Schlafe, was willst du mehr?

   Ewigen Gefühle
   Heben mich hoch und hehr
   Aus irdischem Gewühle,
   Schlafe, was willst du mehr,
   Schlafe, was willst du mehr?

meinem Saitenspiele Segnet der Sterne Heer
Die ewigen Gefühle.

irdischen Gewühle Trennst du mich nur zu sehr,
Bannst mich in diese Kühle;

Schlafe, was willst du mehr, Schlafe, was willst du mehr?
Schlafe, was willst du mehr, Schlafe, was willst du mehr?

2. Die
3. Bannst

mich in die- se Küh- le, Gibst nur im Traum Ge-

-hör! Ach! auf dem wei- chen Pfüh- le

Schla- fe, was willst du mehr? Schla- fe,

schla- fe, was willst du mehr?

[16] Wer sich der Einsamkeit ergibt

Arnold Mendelssohn

Lyrics:
Wer sich der Ein-sam-keit er-gibt, Ach! der ist bald al-lein, Ein Je-der lebt, ein Je-der liebt Und

läßt ihn sei- ner Pein, _____ sei- ner Pein.

Ja laßt mich mei- ner Qual _____ Und kann ich nur ein- mal _____ Recht ein- sam __ sein, Dann bin ich nicht _____ al-

73

42
Qual.
Ach werd' ich erst ein-
f
dim.
pp
p
46
-mal,
Ach werd' ich erst ein- mal,
Ein- sam im
cresc.
dim.
49
Gra- be sein,
Da läßt sie mich al-
p
più dim.
pp
53
-lein.
mf
dim.
rit.
pp

[17] Am Flusse

Arnold Mendelssohn

Langsam, doch nicht schleppend

Ver-flie-ßet, viel-ge-lieb-te Lie-der, Zum Mee-re der Ver-ges-sen-heit! Kein Kna-be sing' ent-

-zückt euch wieder, Kein Mädchen in der Blütenzeit, Kein Mädchen in der Blütenzeit. Ihr

25
san- get nur von mei- ner
fp
fp
fp cresc.
28
più f
Lie- ben; Nun spricht sie mei- ner Treu- e
f
cresc.
31
p
Hohn. Ihr wart ins
ff
p

Was- ser ein- ge- schrie- ben, So

fließt denn auch mit ihm da-

-von, So flie- ßet auch mit

ihm _____ da- von.

Ver- flie-

ßet!

[18] Lied des Mephistopheles

Ferruccio Busoni

Vivace moderato

Es war einmal ein König,
Der hatt' einen großen Floh,
Den liebt' er gar nicht wenig,
Als wie seinen eigenen Sohn.
Da rief er seinen Schneider,
Der

Schnei-der kam her- an: Da, miß dem Jun- ker Klei- der Und miß ihm Ho- sen an. In Sam-met und in Sei- de War er, war er nun an- ge-

-tan, Hatte Bänder auf dem Kleide, Hatt' auch ein Kreuz daran, Und war sogleich Minister Und hatt einen großen Stern. Da wurden seine Geschwister Bei Hof auch große Herrn.

Und Herrn und Fraun am Hofe, Die warn', die waren sehr geplagt, Die Kön'gin und die Zofe Gestochen und genagt, Und

84

49

durf- ten sie nicht knik- ken und

51

weg sie juk- ken nicht. Wir

53

knik- ken und er- stik- ken Doch

55

gleich, wenn ei- ner sticht,

cresc.

Wir knik- ken, er- stik- ken

Doch gleich, wenn ei- ner sticht, Wir

knik- ken und er- stik ken, Wir knik- ken und er-

-stik- ken, wenn ei- ner sticht.

[19] Mailied

Hans Pfitzner

Bewegt, froh, nicht leidenschaftlich *(später sehr steigernd)*

Wie herr- lich leuch- tet Mir die Na- -tur! Wie glänzt die Son- ne! Wie lacht die Flur! Es drin- gen Blü- ten Aus je- dem Zweig

Und tausend Stimmen Aus dem Gesträuch.

Und Freud' und Wonne Aus jeder Brust O Erd', o Sonne! O Glück, o Lust!

O Lieb', o Lie- be!
immer ff
dim.
So gol- den schön, Wie Mor- gen- wol- ken
cresc.
(langsames arpeggio)
Auf je- nen Höh'n! Du seg- nest herr- lich Das fri- sche
Feld, Im Blü- ten- dam- pfe Die vol- le

Welt, Im Blü- ten- dam- pfe Die vol- le Welt. O Mäd- chen, Mäd- chen, Wie lieb' ich dich! Wie blinkt dein Au- ge! Wie liebst du mich!

(Wieder leicht bewegt)

So liebt die Lerche Gesang und Luft,
Und Morgenblumen Den Himmelsduft,
Wie ich dich liebe Mit warmem Blut,
Die du mir Jugend Und Freud' und Mut
Zu neuen

(nicht mehr eilen!)

Lie- dern Und Tän- zen gibst. Sei e- wig glück- lich, Wie du mich liebst!

Sei e- wig glück- lich, wie du mich liebst!

[20] An den Mond

Justus Hermann Wetzel

Fül- lest wie- der Busch und Tal Still mit Ne-bel-glanz, Lö- sest end-lich auch ein--mal Mei- ne See- le ganz. Brei- test ü- ber mein Ge- fild Lin- - dernd dei-nen Blick, Wie des Freun- des _ Au- ge mild

Ü- ber mein _ Ge- schick. Je- den _ Nach- klang fühlt mein Herz _

Froh _ und _ trü- ber _ Zeit, Wand- le zwi-schen Freud _____

_____ und _ Schmerz _ In der Ein- sam- keit. _

Fließe, fließe lieber Fluß! Nimmer werd' ich froh, So verrauschte Scherz und Kuß, Und die Treue so. Ich besaß es doch einmal, Was so köstlich ist! Daß man doch zu seiner Qual Nimmer es vergißt!

Rau-sche, Fluß, das Tal ent-lang, Oh- ne Rast und Ruh, Rau-sche, flü-stre mei-nem Sang Me-lo- di- en zu, Wenn du in der Win-ter-nacht Wü- tend ü- ber- schwillst, O- der um die Früh- ling-spracht Jun- ger Kno-spen quillst.

Se- lig, wer sich vor der Welt Oh- ne Haß ver- schließt, Ei- nen Freund am Bu- sen hält Und mit dem ge- nießt, Was von Men- schen nicht ge- wußt O- der nicht be- dacht, Durch das La- by- rinth der Brust Wan- delt in der Nacht.

[21] Geweihter Platz

Nikolay Karlovich Medtner

Wenn zu den Rei- hen der Nym- phen ver-sam-melt in hei- li- ger Mond- nacht Sich die Gra- zi en heim- lich her-

-ab vom O- lym- pus ge- sel- len

a tempo

[a tempo] poco vivo e più forte

(vivo) calmando

Hier be- lauscht sie der Dich- ter und hört die schö- nen Ge-

calando *pp* *poco mobile*

[*] legatissimo e con Pedale

tranquillo p

-sän- ge

p grazioso

Sieht verschwiegener Tänze geheimnißvolle Bewegung.

Was der Himmel nur herrliches hat, was glücklich die Erde Reizendes immer gebar.

Das er-scheint dem wa-chen-den Träu-mer.

Al-les er-zählt er den Mu-sen und daß die Göt-ter nicht zür-nen Leh-ren die Mu-sen ihn gleich be-schei-den

Ge- heim- nis- se spre- chen.

[22] Rastlose Liebe

Othmar Schoeck

Schnell und stürmisch

Dem Schnee, dem Regen, Dem Wind entgegen, Im Dampf der Klüfte, Durch Nebeldüfte, Immer zu! Immer zu! Ohne Rast und Ruh!

Lieber durch Leiden

Möcht' ich mich schla- gen, Als so viel Freu- den Des Le- bens er- tra- gen. Al- le das Nei- gen Von Her- zen zu Her- zen, Ach, wie so ei- gen Schaf- fet das Schmer- zen!

Wie soll ich fliehen? Wälderwärts ziehen? Alles vergebens! Krone des Lebens,

105

Glück oh- ne Ruh,

Lie- be, bist du!

poco rall. *string.*

Lie- be, bist du!